how to be better at writing....

reports and proposals

atrick Forsyth

The
Industrial
Society

First published in 1997

Apart from any fair dealing for the purposes of research or private study, or criticism or review, as permitted under the Copyright, Designs and Patents Act, 1988, this publication may only be reproduced, stored or transmitted, in any form or by any means, with the prior permission in writing of the publishers, or in the case of reprographic reproduction in accordance with the terms and licences issued by the CLA. Enquiries concerning reproduction outside those terms should be sent to the publishers at the undermentioned address:

Kogan Page Limited
120 Pentonville Road
London N1 9JN

© Patrick Forsyth, 1997

The right of Patrick Forsyth to be identified as author of this work has been asserted by him in accordance with the Copyright, Designs and Patents Act 1988.

British Library Cataloguing in Publication Data
A CIP record for this book is available from the British Library.

ISBN 0 7494 2200 9

Phototypeset by Intype London Ltd
Printed in England by Clays Ltd, St Ives plc

how to better at writing ...

reports and proposals

THE INDUSTRIAL SOCIETY

The Industrial Society stands for changing people's lives. In nearly eighty years of business, the Society has a unique record of transforming organisations by unlocking the potential of their people, bringing unswerving commitment to best practice and tempered by a mission to listen and learn from experience.

The Industrial Society's clear vision of ethics, excellence and learning at work has never been more important. Over 10,000 organisations, including most of the companies that are household names, benefit from corporate Society membership.

The Society works with these, and non-member organisations, in a variety of ways – consultancy, management and skills training, in-house and public courses, information services and multi-media publishing. All this with the single vision – to unlock the potential of people and organisations by promoting ethical standards, excellence and learning at work.

If you would like to know more about the Industrial Society please contact us.

The Industrial Society
48 Bryanston Square
London
W1H 7LN
Telephone 0171 262 2401

The Industrial Society is a Registered Charity No. 290003

CONTENTS

HOW TO BE A BETTER . . . SERIES

Whether you are in a management position or aspiring to one, you are no doubt aware of the increasing need for self-improvement across a wide range of skills.

In recognition of this and sharing their commitment to management development at all levels, Kogan Page and the Industrial Society have joined forces to publish the How to be a Better . . . series.

Designed specifically with your needs in mind, the series covers all the core skills you need to make your mark as a high-performing and effective manager.

Enhanced by mini case studies and step-by-step guidance, the books in the series are written by acknowledged experts who impart their advice in a practical way which encourages effective action.

Now you can bring your management skills up to scratch *and* give your career prospects a boost with the How to be a Better . . . series!

Titles available are:
How to be Better at Giving Presentations
How to be a Better Problem Solver
How to be a Better Interviewer
How to be a Better Teambuilder
How to be Better at Motivating People
How to be a Better Decision Maker
How to be a Better Negotiator
How to be a Better Project Manager
How to be a Better Communicator
How to be Better at Writing Reports and Proposals
How to be Better at Creativity
How to Hold Better Meetings

Forthcoming titles are:
How to be a Better Time Manager

Available from all good booksellers. For further information on the series, please contact:

Kogan Page, 120 Pentonville Road, London N1 9JN
Tel: 0171 278 0433 Fax: 0171 837 6348

For Jacqui:; – (sic) with thanks

ACKNOWLEDGEMENTS

A 'how-to' book such as this cannot be written unaided. Certainly this book draws on much experience and advice from throughout my career. Working, as I have done for more than 20 years, in marketing consultancy and training has made a great deal of writing unavoidable. The work is word-intensive. Reports and proposals; memos and letters; course notes and articles (and, in my case, books); all are an inherent part of the activity.

As I began to get established in my career I quickly realised two things about this element of the work. First, my writing left a bit to be desired. Secondly, it mattered. I became—or was made to become—conscious of what made the process of business writing work. I realised that rules and guidelines did make achieving the desired result more certain; so too did some study of the matter.

So, thanks are due to those of my colleagues who have focused my mind on the problem and the opportunities, and to those clients who have provided feedback over the years. Also to those who have attended courses I have conducted on topics involving writing skills—always their comments and suggestions contribute to any future ability I may have to comment on such matters.

Patrick Forsyth
Touchstone Training & Consultancy
17 Clocktower Mews
London N1 7BB

January 1997

ACKNOWLEDGMENTS

INTRODUCTION

Writing is easy, all you do is sit staring at a blank sheet of paper until the drops of blood form on your forehead

Gene Fowler

In a busy business life writing anything can be a chore. There are surely more important things to be done. People to meet, decisions to be made, action to be taken. Yet all of these things and more can be dependent on written communication. A letter or memo may set up a meeting, a report may present a case and prompt a decision, a proposal may act persuasively to make sure certain action is taken or a particular option is selected. Reading business papers can be a chore also, and they will not achieve their purpose unless they are read, understood and do their job well enough to prompt the reader to action. Business writing must *earn* a reading.

You are probably both a reader and a writer of business documents. Consider writing with your reader's hat on for a moment. Do you read everything that crosses your desk? Do you read every word of the things you do read? Do you read everything from the first word through in sequence, or do you dip into things? Almost certainly the answers make it clear that not all writing is treated equally. Some documents are more likely to be read than others. Of course, some subjects demand your attention. Who ignores a personal note from the managing director? But the fact that some things have to be read does not make their reading any easier or more pleasurable.

Good writing, which means, not least, something that is easy to read and understand, will always be likely to get more attention than sloppy writing. Yet prevailing standards in this area are by no means universally good. I suspect that if I was given a pound for everyone in the world who, as I type this, is struggling through some document and wishing it was better written, I would not need to be writing!

Why is this? Maybe it is education; or lack of it. Certainly little I did at school assisted me with the kind of writing I found myself having to do once I was in business. Maybe it is lack of feedback; perhaps managers are too tolerant of what is put in front of them. If more of it was rejected and had to be rewritten, then more attention might be brought to bear on the task.

Habits are important here too. We all develop a style of writing and may find it difficult to shift away from it. Worse, bad habits may be reinforced by practice. For example, in one computer company where I was asked to conduct a course on proposal writing, I was sent a number of currently typical proposals that seemed to me largely gobbledegook. Asked why they were put together as they were, it became clear that all that had happened was that one proposal had been used as a model for the next; this had continued for six years! During that time no one had really thought about the style of document being used at all. It took a new manager to realise that the rate of strike in terms of new orders was being influenced negatively by the low standard involved.

A FRAGILE PROCESS

We can all recognise the really bad report, without structure or style, but with an excess of jargon, convoluted sentences and which prompts the thought: 'What is it trying to say?' However, such documents do not have to be a complete mess to fail in their purpose. They are inherently fragile. One wrongly chosen word may dilute understanding or act to remove what would otherwise be a positive impression made.

Even something as simple as a spelling mistake (and, no, spell checkers are not infallible) may have a negative effect. I will never forget, in my first year in a consulting firm, playing a small part in proposals that were submitted to a dairy products company. After meetings, deliberations and more meetings a written proposal was sent. A week passed. Then an envelope arrived from the company concerned. Inside was a single sheet of paper. It was a copy of the title page of the proposal and on it was written, in red ink the three words 'No thank you'; this alongside a red ring drawn around one typed word. The word 'Dairy' had been spelt 'Diary'. For a long while after that everything was checked much more carefully.

As a very first rule to drum into your subconscious—check, check and check again. I treasure the computer manual which states, 'The information presented in this publication has been carefully for reliability'; no one is infallible, but I digress.

Whether the cause of a document being less good than it should be is major or minor, the damage is the same. Yet sometimes, despite recognising poor writing when they see it, people may believe that writing habits cannot be changed. I am not sure why. I do a great deal of work in presentation skills training and people rarely doubt that that skill can be improved by training. Yet with writing they do.

A MAJOR OPPORTUNITY

No matter. Whatever the reasons for poor writing may be, suffice to say that if prevailing standards are low then there is a major opportunity here for those who better that standard. More so for those who excel. Business writing is what I call a 'career' skill. It is not only important in a job, and to the undertaking of specific tasks, it is important to the individual. Bad reports might just come back to haunt you later and, just as with certain other skills, progress in an organisation or a career may be dependent on a minimum quality of performance of such tasks.

Recently, I commented on the enthusiasm of a group on an in-company course for the topic and was told by the manager who had set up the event: 'No one gets promoted in this organisation unless they can make a good presentation and write a good report'. Sensible enough and, I suspect, increasingly common.

So, business writing, and particularly the writing of longer documents—the reports and proposals with which this book is concerned—is a vital skill. There may be a great deal hanging on a document doing the job it is intended to do: a decision, a sale, a financial result or a personal reputation. For those who can acquire sound skills in this area very real opportunities exist. The more you have to write, and the more important the documents you create, the more true this is. Quite simply, if you write well then you are more likely to achieve your business goals.

And you can write well. We may not all aspire to or succeed in writing the great novel, but most people can learn to turn out good business writing. Writing that is well tailored to its purpose and likely to create the effect it intends. This book reviews some of the approaches that can make writing reports and proposals easier, quicker (a worthwhile end in itself), and, most important, that makes them more likely to achieve their purpose.

Good business writing need not be difficult, it is a skill which can be developed with study and practice. Some effort may be involved, and certainly practice helps, but it could be worse. Somerset Maugham is quoted as saying: *'There are three rules for writing the novel. Unfortunately, no one knows what they are'*. Business writing is not so dependent on creativity, though this is involved, and it *is* subject to certain rules. Rules, of course, are made to be broken but they do act as useful guidelines and therefore can be a help. This book reviews how to go about the task and, in part, when to follow the rules and when to break them.

Many of the points that follow relate to both reports and proposals, any special points regarding the persuasive nature of proposals are reserved for their own chapter; any overlap is intentional.

1

WHAT MAKES GOOD BUSINESS WRITING?

Despite predictions about the 'paperless office' we seem as sur-rounded—submerged?—by paper as ever. Indeed as documentation is essentially only a form a communication, this is likely to remain so. However a case is presented, even if there is no paper, as with something sent through e-mail for example, it has to be written.

With no communication any organisation is stifled. Without communication nothing much would happen. Communi-cation—good communication—should oil the wheels of organisational activity and facilitate action. This is true of even the simplest memo, and is certainly so of something longer and more complex like a report.

THE HAZARDS OF COMMUNICATION

Communication is—inherently—not straightforward. Perhaps this is an understatement: communication can be downright difficult. We all know this and experience it day to day. How often in your office do people say: 'What exactly do you mean?', 'Why ever didn't you say so?', 'Don't you understand any-thing?', 'Listen, for goodness sake, listen'. Confusion in all its forms is a constant lurking presence.

Confusion may occur after just a few words. What *exactly* is '24-hour service', other than insufficiently spelt out? When exactly can we expect something someone says they will do 'right away'? If this is true of such tiny communications, how much more potential for misunderstanding does a 25-page report present?

Much of the confusion arising from unclear communication is the result of lack of thought. In discussion, the old adage that we should 'engage the brain before opening the mouth' is a good one. Yet in conversation at least the opportunity to sort things out is there. A question can be asked, a clarification given and the conversation can then proceed with everyone clear what was meant. But with written communication the danger is that the confusion lasts. There is not necessarily an immediate opportunity to check (the writer might be a hundred miles away), and a misunderstanding on page 3 may skew the whole message taken from an entire report.

So, the first requirement of good business writing is clarity. I make no apology for the fact that I return to this more than once through this book. A good report needs thinking about if it is to be clear, and it should never be taken for granted that understanding will be automatically generated by what we write.

It is more likely that we will give due consideration to clarity, and give the attention it needs to achieving it, if we are clear about the purpose of any report we may write.

WHY HAVE A REPORT?

Exactly why a report is written is important. This may seem self evident, yet many reports are no more than something 'about' their topic. Their purpose is not clear. Without clear intentions the tendency is for the report to ramble, to go round and round and not come to any clear conclusion.

Reports may be written for many reasons, for example they may intend to:

❑ inform;
❑ recommend;

❏ motivate;
❏ prompt or play a part in debate;
❏ persuade;
❏ impress;
❏ record;
❏ reinforce or build on existing situations or beliefs;
❏ instruct.

In addition, they may have more complex objectives such as changing people's attitudes. Further, such factors are not mutually exclusive. You may need to do a number of things simultaneously. Or you may need to do some things for one group of people and others for different groups. A report designed to explain an organisational change, and set implementation in train, may need to pick up and develop a situation of which senior people are generally aware and yet start from scratch with others. The first group may be already persuaded that the change is good, and are eager for the details. The others may be deeply suspicious.

Any such complexity compounds the problem of writing an appropriate report: recognising and understanding such complexities, and seeing any inherent conflicts that may affect the way a report is received, is the first step to being able to produce something that will do the job required and do it well.

READER EXPECTATIONS

If a report is to be well received, then it must meet certain expectations of its readers. Before going into these let us consider generally what conditions such expectations. Psychologists talk about what they call 'cognitive cost'. This is best explained by example. Imagine you are wanting to programme the video recorder. You want to do something that is other than routine, so you get out the instruction book. Big mistake. You open it (try this, you can open it at random) and the two-page spread shouts at you 'This is going to be difficult!' Such a document has a high cognitive cost, rather than appearing inviting, even a cursory look is off-putting.

People are wary of this effect. They look at any document almost *expecting* reading it to be hard work. If they discover it looks easier and more inviting than they thought (a low cognitive cost), then they are likely to read it with more enthusiasm. What gives people the feeling, both at first glance and as they get further into it, that a report is not to be avoided on principle? In no particular order, the following are some of the key factors. They like it if it is:

❑ **Brief**: obviously something shorter is likely to appear to be easier to read than something long, but what really matters is that a report is of an appropriate length for its topic and purpose. Perhaps the best word to apply is '*succinct*': to the point, long enough to say what is necessary and no more. A report may be 10 pages long or 50 and still qualify for this description.

❑ **Clear**: they must be able to understand it. This applies in a number of ways; for example, it should be clearly written (in the sense of not being convoluted), and use appropriate language—you should not feel that, as an intended reader, you have to look up every second word in a dictionary.

❑ **Precise**: saying exactly what is necessary and not constantly digressing without purpose.

❑ **In 'our language'**: in other words using a level and style of language that is likely to make sense to the average reader, and which displays evidence of being designed to do so.

❑ **Simple**: avoiding unnecessary complexity (something we will return to in Chapter 4).

❑ **Well structured**: so that it proceeds logically through a sequence that is clear and makes sense as a sensible way of dealing with the message.

❑ **Descriptive**: again we return to this in Chapter 4; here it suffices to say that if there is a need to paint a picture it must do so in a way that gets that picture over.

All these have in common that they can act to make reading

easier. Further, they act cumulatively, that is the more things that are right in each of these ways, the clearer the overall report will be. If the impression is given that attention has *actively* been given to making the reader's task easier, so much the better.

EXERCISE

Both the above factors are worth personalising to the kind of people to whom you must write. Whether this is internal, eg colleagues or external, eg customers or collaborators, you need to be clear what your communications have to do and what kind of expectations exist at the other end. For example, a technical person may have different expectations from a layperson, and may be looking to check a level of detail that must exist and be expressed clearly for the report to be acceptable to them.

Make a list of typical recipients of your documents and what they expect, to keep by you as you write.

THE READERS' PERSPECTIVE

It follows logically from what has been said in this chapter so far that a good report must reflect the needs of the reader. Report writing cannot be undertaken in a vacuum. It is not simply an opportunity for the writer to say things as he or she wants. Ultimately a report can only be judged good by its readers. Thus their perspective is the starting-point and as the report writer you need to think about who the intended readers are, how they think, how they view the topic of the report, what their experience to date is of the issues, and how they are likely to react to what you have to say. This links to preparation which is dealt with in depth in the next chapter.

All this is surely no more than common sense, yet it must be easy to forget or there would not be so many turgid reports around and so many disillusioned report readers. How so? First, it is all too easy to find you are taking a somewhat introspective view in putting something down on paper. After all, you view yourself as important, you are involved, you are knowledgeable about the matter, why else are you the person writing the report?

Secondly, many people have been dropped into business writing at the deep end. One day someone requested a report, and you crept off to find something similar which you could use as a template. This is fine if what was picked up was a first-class document; if not it is like the blind leading the blind.

POWERFUL HABITS

The result of any initial bad experience may well have been to develop bad habits. The new report writer quickly gets into a particular way of presenting material and much of it then becomes a reflex. This may become something that allows failure by default. Reports fail to present a clear case, people find reading them tedious and frustrating and whatever it is they aim to do (prompt a decision, perhaps) fails to occur.

Habit, and the pressure of business, combine to push people into writing on 'automatic pilot'. Sometimes if you critique something that you wrote, or that went out from your department, you can clearly see something that is wrong. A sentence does not make sense, a point fails to get across or a description confuses rather than clarifies. Usually the reason this has occurred is not that the writer really thought this was the best sentence or phrase and got it wrong. Rather it was because there was inadequate thought of any sort; or none at all.

Habits can be difficult to break and the end result can be a plethora of material moving around organisations couched in a kind of gobbledegook or what some call 'officespeak'. The example in Figure 1.1 is a caricature of this sort of communication, but there is too much in circulation that comes too close to this.

STANDARD PROGRESS REPORT
(for those with no progress to report)

During the survey period which ended on 14 February, considerable progress has been made in the preliminary work directed towards the establishment of the initial activities. (*We are getting ready to start, but we have not done anything yet.*) The background information has been reviewed and the functional structure of the various component parts of the project have been matched with appropriate human resources. (*We looked at the project and decided George should lead it.*)

Considerable difficulty has been encountered in the selection of optimum approaches and methods, but this problem is being attacked vigorously and we expect the development phase will proceed at a satisfactory rate. (*George is reading the brief.*) In order to prevent the unnecessary duplication of previous work in the same field, it was necessary to establish a project team which has conducted a quite extensive tour through various departments with immediate relevance to the study. (*George and Mary had a nice time visiting everyone.*)

The Steering Committee held its regular meetings and considered quite important policy matters pertaining to the overall organisational levels of the line and staff responsibilities that devolve on the personnel associated with the specific assignments resulting from the broad functional specifications. (*Which means . . .?*) It is believed that the rate of progress will continue to accelerate as necessary personnel become available to play their part in the discussions that must precede decisions. (*We really will do something soon—if we can.*)

Figure 1.1 *From the company notice board*

EARNING A READING

The moral here is clear. Good report writing does not just happen. It needs some thought and some effort (and some study, with which this book aims to assist). The process needs to be actively worked at if the result is going to do the job you have in mind, and do it with some certainty.

Good habits are as powerful as bad ones. A shift from one to another is possible and the rewards in this case make the effort particularly worthwhile. Think what good report writing skills can achieve.

THE REWARDS OF EXCELLENCE

Occasionally reports may be written 'for the record'. They are of no great import or value. More often, however, if trouble is being taken to prepare a report then it has some real purpose. Reports are written to lead to action, to make things happen, or play a part in so doing. Communication influences people, and here the intention is clear: a report usually has a case to present, one that will act so as to play a part in the thinking that follows. A decision is made, albeit in part, because of the way the case has been put over in a report.

So far so good: reports can influence action. However, they also act to create an image of the writer. Within an organisation of any size, people interact through communication. They send each other memos, they sit in meetings and on committees, they chat as they pass on the stairs, or share a sandwich at lunchtime; and all of this sends out signals. It tells the world, or at least the organisation, something about them. Are they knowledgeable, competent, expert, easy to deal with, decisive—would you take their advice, follow their lead or support their cause?

All the different ways in which people interrelate act together, cumulatively and progressively, to build up and maintain an image of each individual. Some ways may play a dispro-portionate part, and report writing is one such. There are two reasons why this effect is important. First, reports, unlike more transient means of communication, can last. They are passed around, considered and remain on the record; more so if they are about important issues. Secondly, because not everyone can write a good report, people can be impressed by a clear ability to marshal an argument and put it over in writing.

Thus reports represent an opportunity, or in fact two opportunities. Reports—at least, good ones—can be instrumental in prompting action; action you want, perhaps. They are also important to your profile. They say something about the kind of person you are and how you are to work with. In a sense there are situations where you want to make sure certain personal qualities shine through. A case may be supported by it being clear it is presented by someone who gives attention to details, for instance.

The view taken of someone by their superiors in the longer term may be influenced by their regularly reading what they regard as good reports. So, next time you are burning the midnight oil to get some seemingly tedious report finalised, think of it as the business equivalent of an open goal and remember, it could literally be affecting your chances of promotion!

A SIGNIFICANT OPPORTUNITY

Reports demand detailed work. Their preparation may, on occasion, seem tedious. They certainly need adequate time set aside for them. But as the old saying has it: if a job is worth doing, it is worth doing well. It may take no more time to prepare a good report than it does to prepare a lacklustre one. Indeed, the next chapter contends that a systematic approach can speed up your writing.

If reports, and other such documentation, are clear, focused and set out to earn a reading they are more likely to achieve their purpose. In this case they are also more likely to act positively to enhance the profile of the writer. Both these results are surely worthwhile. But the job still has to be done, the words still have to be got down on paper, and faced with a blank sheet (or, these days, screen) this can be a daunting task (I know—at this point

I still have five chapters in front of me!). Making writing easier starts with preparation, and it is to this we turn in the next chapter.

KEY POINTS

❏ Remember: communication has inherent dangers; clear communication needs to be well considered.

❏ Reports will only achieve their purpose if the writer is clear in his or her own mind what he or she is seeking to achieve.

❏ The reader is more important than the writer; write for others not for yourself.

❏ Beware of old habits and work to establish good ones.

❏ Reports are potentially powerful tools—powerful in action terms, and powerful in contributing to personal profile.

CREATING A GOOD REPORT

In this chapter, ahead of considering anything about the actual process of getting words on to paper, we look at the construction or the 'shape' of a good report. There are two considerations here:

1. What makes it work for the reader?
2. What assists you to compile it quickly and easily?

Of these, the first is the most important, but the factors involved luckily act positively in both cases. The starting-point to thinking here is clear.

SETTING CLEAR OBJECTIVES

The most important thing to settle initially is simply *why* the report is being written. What is it *for*? Few reports are just 'about' something. They may, of course, have various intentions: to inform, motivate and so on, as mentioned in the last chapter. What matters most is the overall **objective**. This in turn means that you must be clear what you want the end result to be after the report is delivered and read.

For example, it is unlikely to be a clear objective to write something 'about the possibility of the office relocating'. It may be valid to write something to explain why this may be necessary, compare the relative merits of different solutions and recommend the best option. Even that may need more specifics within it, spelling out the advantages/disadvantages to different

---

groups: staff, customers etc, who may each be affected in different ways.

Objectives should be defined from the standpoint of the readers. You need to consider:

❑ which particular people the report is for;
❑ whether the group is homogeneous or if multiple needs must be met;
❑ the reasons these people want the report;
❑ what they want in it, and in what detail;
❑ what they do *not* want; and
❑ the result they look for (what do they want to understand, what action do they want to take, or what decision do they want to be able to make?).

It follows that it may well help to know something about the recipients of any report that you write. You may, of course, know them well; for example, they may be colleagues with whom you work closely. If not, ask yourself:

❑ What kind of people are they? (e.g. male/female, young/old)

✎

_____

_____

_____

❑ How well do you know them?

✎

_____

_____

_____

❑ What is their experience of the report's topic?

_____

_____

_____

❑ What is their level of knowledge regarding the topic?

_____

_____

_____

❑ What is their likely attitude to it? (e.g. welcoming/hostile)

_____

_____

_____

❑ What is their personal involvement? (i.e. how do the issues affect them?)

_____

_____

_____

❑ How do they rank the importance of the topic?

_____

_____

_____

❑   Are they likely to find the topic interesting?

✎

_____

_____

_____

❑   Are they likely to act as a result of reading it?

✎

_____

_____

_____

Everything that follows, what you write, how you write it and how you arrange it, is dependent on this first premiss: a clear objective is literally the foundation on which a good report is based. We will return to this, and to exactly how you set such an objective, in considering preparation for writing in the next chapter. Meantime we turn to the actual shape of the report itself.

A SOUND STRUCTURE

The simplest structure one can imagine is a beginning, a middle and an end. Indeed this is what a *report* must consist of, but the *argument* or case it presents may be somewhat more complex. This falls naturally into four parts:

1.   Setting out the **situation**.
2.   Describing the **implications**.
3.   Reviewing the **possibilities**.
4.   Making a **recommendation**.

The two structures can coexist comfortably, as shown in Figure 2.1.

An example helps to spell out the logical way an argument needs to be presented if it is to be got over clearly. Imagine

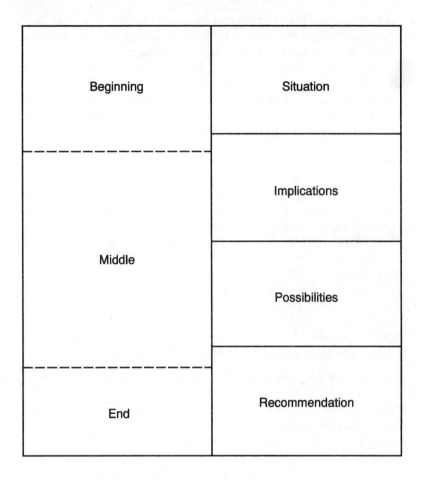

Figure 2.1 *The two structures of a report*

an organisation with certain communication problems; a report making suggestions to correct this might follow the following broad sequence:

1. **The situation:** this might refer to both the quantity and importance of written communication around, and outside, the organisation. Also to the fact that writing skills were poor, and

no standards were in operation, nor had any training ever been done to develop skills or link them to recognised models that would be acceptable around the organisation.

2. **The implications:** these might range from a loss of productivity (because documents took too long to create and had constantly to be referred back for clarification), to inefficiencies or worse resulting from misunderstood communications. It could also include dilution or damage to image because of poor documents circulating outside the organisation, perhaps to customers.

3. **The possibilities:** here, as with any argument, there might be many possible courses of action, all with their own mix of pros and cons. To continue the example, it might range from limiting report writing to a small core group of people, to reducing paperwork completely or setting up a training programme and subsequent monitoring system to ensure some improvement took place.

4. **The recommendation:** here the 'best' option needs to be set out. Or, in some reports, a number of options must be reviewed from which others can choose. Recommendations need to be specific: addressing exactly what should be done, by whom and when, alongside such details as cost and logistics.

At all stages generalisations should be avoided. Reports should contain facts, evidence and sufficient 'chapter and verse' for those in receipt of them to see them as an appropriate basis for decision or action.

With the overall shape of the argument clearly in mind we can look in more detail at the shape of the report itself. The way in which it flows through from the beginning to the end is intended to carry the argument, make it easy to follow and to read, and to make it interesting too, as necessary, along the way.

The three parts fit, unsurprisingly, the old and useful maxim about communications usually abbreviated to: 'Tell 'em, tell 'em and tell 'em'. In full this says: tell people what you are going to tell them—*the introduction*; tell them in detail—*the body of the report*; and then tell them what you have told them—or *summarise*.

FIRST, THE BEGINNING

This must start by addressing the stance of the readers. What will they be thinking as they start reading? *Will it be interesting? Readable? Will it help me? Is it important?* Will it distract them from anything else going on around them, engaging their concentration so that they give it their attention.

They have their own agenda, wanting it to be succinct etc as mentioned earlier; essentially they will only give it real consideration if they find it understandable, interesting and a good fit with their situation. They do **not** want to find it inappropriate. It should not: confuse them, blind them with science/technicalities or jargon, lose them in an impenetrable structure (or lack of it), or talk down to them.

Judgements are made very quickly. In the first few lines a view is adopted that colours their reading of the rest of the document. 'First impressions last', as the old saying has it, so this stage is very important and may need disproportionate thought to get it phrased and constructed just right.

The beginning must act as an introduction, which must:

❏ set the scene (this can include linking to terms of reference or past discussions that prompted the report to be written);
❏ state the topic and theme (and maybe treatment);
❏ make the objectives clear;
❏ begin to get into the topic, creating a thread that helps to draw the reader through the first part to the core of the report;
❏ position itself as appropriate for the readers (who must not feel they are, as it were, eavesdropping on something meant for others).

At the same time, the beginning will inevitably say something about the writer, and therefore needs to reflect anything you want readers to feel (that you are expert, professional or whatever) and not put out any untoward messages (too much jargon may say 'this person does not understand the needs of their readers'). So this element must be injected, something we return to in Chapter 4.

If it is to earn a reading a report must get quickly to the point. This does not preclude setting the scene. A report might start: 'This report sets out to demonstrate how the organisation can cut costs by 10 per cent, without sacrificing quality'. After this, and perhaps a little more, has got readers wanting to know how, it may be necessary to go back and set the scene in terms that reflect an analysis of current expenditure. However, people know where it is going—they will go through the text more easily once a desirable intention has been spelt out.

The tone of a report also needs to show itself at this first stage. Just as presenters need to establish rapport with their audiences, so a report receives continuing attention if it comes over as necessary; useful, written for a purpose, written with conviction, written by someone to whom the readers want to listen; and, above all, written with understanding of, and concern for, its readers.

Get off to a good start and any continuing task is then often easier. This certainly applies to writing. Feeling you have got a good beginning breeds confidence in what must follow. So too with reading: if a document starts well, people read on, wanting the rest to match the early acceptability. There are plenty of frustrations in corporate life; something that looks set to make life a little easier is very soon recognised and appreciated.

One of the reasons that what is often called **the executive summary** (a summary placed at the beginning rather than the end) often works well, is that it meets many of the criteria for the beginning now stated. It interests the reader who then reads on to discover the detail and see how and why the stated conclusions have been arrived at. The question of summaries is reviewed further in Chapter 6.

THE MIDDLE

This is the core of the document. It is where the greatest amount of the content is to be found, and hence it has the greatest need for structure and organisation. The key aims here are to:

❑ put over the detail of the report's message;
❑ maintain, indeed develop, interest;
❑ ensure clarity and a manner appropriate to the reader.

It may be necessary to go further. It is here that the report may seek acceptance and, conversely, set out to counter people disagreeing with or rejecting what it has to say. At the same time any complexity must be kept manageable. Doing this necessitates the simple practice of taking one point at a time. So here, attempting to practise what I preach, are a number of points all aimed at keeping this core section on track. First, matters to do with:

Putting over the content

❑ **A logical structure:** selecting, and describing to your readers, a way through the content (for example, describing something in chronological order).
❑ **'Signposting' intentions:** knowing broadly what is coming (and why) makes reading easier. This is why many documents need a contents page, but it can also be done within the text, ie 'We will review the project in terms of three key factors: timing, cost and staffing. First, timing . . .' (perhaps followed by a heading saying: 'Timing'. This is something it is difficult to overdo, the clarity it promotes and the feeling of having what is being read in context of what is to come is appreciated.
❑ **Using headings** (and sub-headings): this is not only effectively a form of signposting, it breaks up the text visually and makes it easier to work through a page (contrast the style of a modern business book, such as this, with the kind of dense textbook many of us suffered at school).
❑ **Appropriate language:** is important at every stage (see Chapter 4).
❑ **Using graphics** (visual graphic devices): this encompasses two types of factor: such things as bold type, capital letters etc; and illustrations: including graphs, tables, charts etc. Both promote clarity and are dealt with in Chapter 6.

Gaining acceptance

This is a discrete aim and can be assisted in a number of ways, for example:

❏ **Relate to specific groups:** general points and argument may not be so readily accepted as those addressed to a specific group. There is no reason why a report cannot do both, with some paragraphs or points addressed generally and others starting with, for example, 'For those new to the organisation' or ' . . . those in the sales department . . .' etc.

❏ **Provide proof:** certainly if acceptance is desired, you need to offer something other than your say-so, especially if you could be seen as having a vested interest of some sort. So such things as opinion, research, statistics and tests from elsewhere will all strengthen your case. Remember there is a link between the acceptability of the source and the force it brings to bear, so you may need to choose carefully exactly how best to make a point.

❏ **Anticipate objections:** there is no merit in ignoring negative points you are sure will come into readers' minds as the report is read, or they will simply invalidate what it says. Such are often better met head on, indeed signposted, ie, 'Some will be asking how . . .? So in the next three paragraphs I will address exactly that.'

The middle section of a report needs to be linked visibly to the beginning and the end. It should pick up neatly from points made in the introduction, especially if they have bearing on structure (which should be consistent throughout). It should link equally neatly to the end. This means the thread of content needs to weave its way throughout the report and across the divide between the three main segments.

The end result is well described as seamless. The content—the case it presents—flows throughout the whole report and everything structural *supports* that rather than *competes* with it. The end result is something essentially readable, and also easy to follow.

One final point is worth adding before proceeding to deal with the end; it is sometimes a nice touch if the text towards the end of the middle acknowledges the stage that has been reached, ie, 'Last, a final point before the summary . . .' as was done in this paragraph.

THE END

First some dangers. Some reports seem to avoid the end. The middle runs out of structure. It deteriorates into something that effectively keeps saying 'and another thing'. This can be distracting and annoying. Beware:

❏ **False endings:** I saw a report not so long ago that had the word finally, albeit used in slightly different ways, three times among the final paragraphs.
❏ **Overshooting the structure:** wandering on beyond the last heading yet failing actually to move into the end section. This can add a paragraph or several pages, and consist of unnecessary repetition or irrelevant digression; all such is a distraction.

So what positively should you do here? The end has three particular intents:

1. To reach and present a **conclusion** (this reflects the type of document involved and the nature of the argument that it may present).
2. To pull together and **summarise** the content.
3. To end **positively**, on a 'high note' or with a flourish. Or, if that is overstating it somewhat (and many reports are on routine matters rather than exciting ones), at least to end with some power and authority, rather than tail away.

Summarising is not the easiest thing to do succinctly and effectively. Precisely because of this, it represents a particular opportunity. If it is done well it impresses. Perversely, this may actually help in getting the report the attention it deserves. Realistically we know that many people glance at the end of a report before deciding to read it through. If the summary is a good sample of what, in that case, is to come then it will reinforce that decision.

A summary develops out of the content most easily if the sequence and structure has been sensible, sound and logical. A summary is, after all, the natural conclusion of many cases. However you summarise, it is inherent to its acceptance that you keep this part of the report comparatively short. This does not necessarily mean only a few lines, it is often the case that a long, complex report will need more than this by way of summary. The important thing is that the summary appears and that it is an appropriate length compared with the whole report. It is the need to make a summary brief as well as to encapsulate the essence of the content and conclusions that make it difficult to compose without some consideration.

The end section is a part of the report where disproportionate time, editing and checking may be useful. Certainly it is a waste to slave at length over a long report, and then allow its effectiveness to be diluted (or at worst destroyed) by inattention to this vital stage.

AFTER THE END

It is worth noting that 'the end' may not be. In other words there may be pages that follow the summary and conclusions. Prime amongst such are appendices, which can be used to take certain discrete areas of detail out of the main core of the content. This may allow them to be dealt with in more detail, but the role of such things is as much to keep the middle manageable and stop it from becoming too long and having its key arguments submerged in endless detail.

CASE STUDY

George had not been too happy to be given the job of organising the office rearrangement. Even though it was for the best of reasons, growth—and higher profit—meant accommodating more people, especially in customer services. He knew many people were a bit worried about how the changes would affect them, so, determined to get things right, he set to with a vengeance.

He was nothing if not thorough. He measured every room, he counted everything that moved and catalogued everything that did not. He mapped every electric wire and noted who used what pieces of equipment. Then he set about writing a report of his findings and suggestions.

Amazed at just how much there was to record, he had the good sense to check his draft with a colleague. They were appalled. People will react badly, they suggested: 'People don't want all that detail, it took me ten minutes to even find where I was going to sit and I still don't know why I am moving—you need to look at it from other people's point of view'.

Chastened, George went 'back to the drawing board'. He rewrote the report, beginning with an overview of how the changes would help the organisation. He set out a brief, clear description of how each department was affected, stressing the advantages. And he made clear what had to be done, by who and when to implement the changes.

Three weeks later, though there were, of course, some questions and a few suspicions, all concerned had been moved without a hitch and everything was running well. But it was nearly so very different.

KEY POINTS

❑ Every good report has clear objectives.

❑ The readers' perspective is more important than the writer's.

❑ There should be a clear, logical structure to the argument (situation, implications, possibilities, recommendations).

❑ There should be a clear shape to the report (beginning, middle and end).

❑ The end result should flow, be readable throughout and be 'seamless'.

3

PREPARING TO WRITE

Knowing you have to write a report can prompt different responses in different people: put if off, doodle, write some central part quickly and ahead of the rest 'because you know that'. Whatever you do now, whatever your current habits are, you might want to consider the exercise below before continuing with this chapter.

EXERCISE

It might be useful, at this point, to have something that you have written beside you as you read on, and to think particularly about *how* it got written. In other words, what procedure and actions, in what order, went into drafting it.

You can do this in three ways:

❏ Wait until you have a drafting job to do, do it, keep a note of how you went about and have it by you as you read on.

❏ Write something (or at least start to) as an exercise and use it as a guideline to your current style and practice.

❏ locate something (preferably recent, so that you still have the details of it in mind) from the files, and make some notes as to how you composed it to keep by you.

Few areas of business skill can be acquired through some magic formula, and report writing is no exception. However, preparation perhaps comes close to acting in this way. It really is the foundation on which successful report writing is based. Preparation allows you to do two things. First, to create a report that not only you feel content with, but one that has a clear purpose and which is regarded as useful by its readers. As has been said, the ultimate measure of a good report is whether it achieves the outcome you wish.

Secondly, a systematic approach to preparation and writing will save you time. This is a worthy result in its own right. Which of us does not have too much to do? When I first had to do a significant volume of writing, and thus looked into what made it work well in order to improve my own practice, the way I worked did change. It was a matter of some surprise to me that, whatever effect this may have had on what I wrote, I found I was getting my writing done more quickly. This experience has been found also by many people I have met through training on this topic; and is, I am sure, something you may find too.

In this chapter, therefore, we review the actual process of preparation and getting the words down. If this is put alongside what was covered in the last chapter about the shape and structure of a report, then together they begin to provide a blueprint to best practice. First things first. We will start with what you should not do.

Do not, faced with the task of writing what looks like being a 20-page report, get out a clean sheet of paper and immediately start writing the first words: '1. Introduction. This report sets out . . .'. Thinking must proceed writing.

WHY THIS REPORT?

Like so much in business, a report needs clear objectives. Let us be specific about that. Objectives are not what you wish to *say*, they are what you wish to *achieve*. Put simply, the task is not to write, say, 'about the new policy', it is to ensure people understand the proposed change and how it is intended to work. This in turn is designed to ensure people accept the necessity for it and are prompted to undertake their future work in a way that fits with the new policy.

Once this is clear in mind the writing is already likely to be easier, and we might move on to specifying that such a report needs to deal with five main topics:

1. Some background to the change.
2. An explanation of why it is necessary (perhaps emphasising the good things to which it will lead).
3. Exactly what it is and how it works.
4. The effects on the individual.
5. What action people need to take.

With a more specific situation in mind (perhaps the topic you took for the exercise above), objectives can be formed precisely if, as the much quoted acronym has it, they are SMART. That is:

❑ Specific
❑ Measurable
❑ Achievable
❑ Realistic, and
❑ Timed.

As an example, imagine you are setting up a training course on the subject of writing reports and proposals. What objectives would you set? The following follows the SMART principle: the course should:

❑ enable participants to ensure future reports are written in a way that will be seen by their readers as appropriate, informative and, above all, readable (*specific*);
❑ ensure (*measurable*) action occurs after the session, eg future proposals might be measured by the number of recipients who subsequently confirmed agreement;
❑ be appropriate for the chosen group, eg an inexperienced group might need a longer and more detailed programme than one comprised of people with more experience; and thus have *achievable* objectives;

❏ be not just achievable but *realistic*, eg here the time away from the job might be compared with the potential results of the course to ensure attendance was desirable;

❏ and be *timed*: When is the workshop—in a month or in six months? How long will it last—one day, two days? Results cannot come until it has taken place.

In addition, objectives should be phrased more in terms of readers than of the writer, and overall the key questions:

❏ **Why** am I writing this?
❏ **What** am I trying to achieve?

must be answered clearly. To check if an answer to either is too vague to be useful, say of it 'which means that . . .' and see if this leads to a more specific statement. For example, you might say simply that such a course is designed to: improve report writing skills. So far so good; but what does this mean? It means that documents will be less time consuming to prepare than in the past, more reader oriented and more likely to achieve their objectives. This line of thinking can be pursued until objectives are absolutely clear.

Once your objectives are set satisfactorily you can proceed to the real business of getting something down on paper, though remember this does not mean starting at the beginning and writing on to the end.

RESEARCH PRIOR TO PREPARATION

It is important to ensure that you are in a position to write the report before you start. This may mean some research. On occasions this is too grand a word for it. You simply need a few moments to collect your thoughts, perhaps to pull together a number of papers and proceed with what that puts in your mind.

The danger is that this is all you do (if that) when research must actually mean something more elaborate and time-consuming. Make no mistake, if it needs to be done, it needs to be done. The time equation here is well proven: more time on research and preparation means less on writing because the writing flows more smoothly. The alternative may be a report which is less effective than you want, or which fails in its purpose.

So let us see what any necessary research means must be done as a specific aspect of overall preparation. The key question to start with is one of information. Ask yourself:

❏ What do you need to know in order to write the report?

✎
_____

_____

_____

Then, to assemble the information, you need to consider sources. This may involve quite a list. So, for example, ask yourself:

❏ Which people do you need to consult (within and without the organisation)?

✎
_____

_____

_____

❏ To which published or written sources do you need to refer (this may include anything from an earlier report, a research study, a book, a magazine or just a memo)?

You may also need to put some order, and specify some order of importance, into the equation. It is certainly not suggested that the first step before writing anything is six months talking, reading and making notes. Only a finite amount of material will be useful, but you may need to cast the net wide initially, at least in terms of considering what might be useful. In this way you can get alongside you the information (opinion, fact, figures, notes, summaries etc) that you will need as you start to write.

Having gathered the information and screened out that which is superfluous, you need to organise it. The easiest way is to arrange it into some appropriate subgroups: everything to do with costs or with timing, say, depending on what the overall subject may be. This makes the task of reviewing the material more manageable, then you can move on with a neat set of materials to hand, rather than a large, random heap.

CASE STUDY

Mary has a report to write and a tight deadline. She knows it is important and also that she cannot do the work without some research. With other pressures looming, and the deadline ever present, she opts for the minimum amount of prior checking and gets down to writing.

Half way through she realises the draft is going off the rails. She has to pause to get some more references, again to talk to one or two colleagues and to spend time on the telephone to an outside agency. The result is that the writing takes place in fits and starts. The flow is difficult to sustain, and despite the right content now being included, with the deadline now upon her she has to send off the document knowing that it could be better.

In fact the lesson is not that some additional revisions would have helped, but that more time up front would have reduced the writing time *and* made the end result better, while still hitting the deadline. Next time she will know better.

A SYSTEMATIC APPROACH

It is a rare person who can create a good report without making a few notes first, and frankly the complexity of many such documents demands a little more than this. Sometimes perhaps all that is necessary is a dozen words on the back of the proverbial envelope, but you need to be very sure that you are not missing anything. Unless you are thoroughly prepared, the chances are that whatever you create as your first draft will be somewhat off target, and time must then be spent tinkering and reworking to get it into order.

Another danger is compounded by deadlines. And who never has to work to tighter deadlines than they would like? Too often skimping preparation, combined with a pressing deadline, means that a report must be submitted even though the writer knows that an additional review and some more editing would make it more likely to do its job well.

So, to encompass all possibilities and degrees of complexity, the following six-stage approach sets out a methodology that will cope with any kind of document (it is the way this book began life too). It is recommended only by its practicality. It works. It will make the job quicker and more certain. It can install the right habits and rapidly becomes something you can work with, utilising its methods more or less comprehensively depending on the circumstances.

The six stages are now reviewed in turn, alongside an example. To provide an example that is straightforward and easy for everyone to relate to, imagine that you have to write something about your job. To make it more interesting, and give it a specific objective, imagine that what needs to be written is to attract internal candidates to apply for your job; because (we can imagine what we like) you are to be promoted once a successful applicant is found.

Stage 1: **Listing**

This consists of ignoring all thoughts about sequence or structure, and simply listing everything—every significant point—which might be desirable or necessary to include (though perhaps bearing in mind the kind of report and level of detail involved).

This, a process that draws on what is sometimes called 'mind-mapping', gets all the elements involved down on paper. It may need more than one session to complete it; certainly you will find one thought leading to another as the picture fills out.

Stage 1: Listing

qualifications

experience   Headline   Department
                                                                            (size, purpose,
                                                                            reputation, developments)

Kind of person — what they <u>can</u> do
              — what they will do

Salary
                            Travel
Benefits
(e.g. car)
                                                        Action — reply
                                                               — c.v.
                                                               — photo
                                                               — interviews
                                                               — deadline

Special characteristics
 — clean driving licence
 — fluent French
 — able to write a good report   Job title

                                    Job objectives ══

                        Main tasks/ responsibilities ──
                                                        ══

Training

Rather than set this out as a neat list down the page, many find it more useful to accommodate the developing picture to adopt a freestyle approach.

In this way points are noted, almost at random, around a sheet. This allows you to end up able to view the totality of your notes in one glance, so if it is necessary you should use a sheet larger than standard A4 paper. It is also best done on paper not on screen (the next stages make clear why).

The box relates this stage to the example to show something of what is done.

Stage 2: Sorting

Next, you can proceed to rearrange what you have noted and bring some logic and organisation to bear on it. This process may raise some questions as well as answer others, so it is still not giving you the final shape of the report. This stage is often best (and most quickly) done by annotating the original list. A second colour may help now as you begin to put things in order, make logical groupings and connections, as well as allowing yourself to add and subtract points and refine the total picture as you go.

The example continues in the box.

Stage 3: Arranging

This stage arranges your 'jottings' into a final order of contents, and here you can decide on the precise sequence and arrangements you will follow for the report itself. For the sake of neatness, and thus to give yourself a clear guideline to follow as you move on, it is often worth rewriting the sheet you were left with after stage 2 (indeed, now so many people work directly with keyboard and screen, this is the point to transfer to that if you wish, as what you are creating now is a sequential list).

At this stage you can also form a view and note specifically the emphasis that will be involved. For example: What is most important? Where is most detail necessary? What needs illustrating (this may involve anything from a graph to an anecdote)?

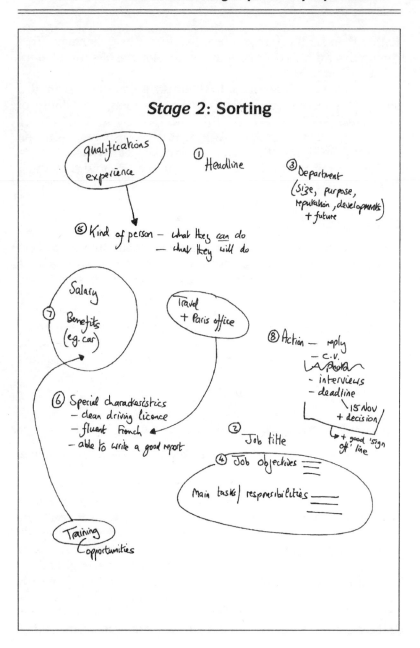

Stage 2: Sorting

qualifications
experience

① Headline

③ Department
(size, purpose,
reputation, developments)
+ future

⑤ Kind of person — what they *can* do
— what they *will* do

Salary

⑦ Benefits
(eg. car)

Travel
+ Paris office

⑧ Action — reply
— c.v.
— photo
— interviews
— deadline
15 Nov
+ decision
+ good 'sign
off' line

⑥ Special characteristics
— clean driving licence
— fluent French
— able to write a good report

② Job title

④ Job objectives ═══

Main tasks / responsibilities ════

Training
opportunities

Stage 3: Arranging

qualifications

experience   Headline   Department
                                                               (size, purpose,
                                                               reputation, developments)

Kind of person – what they <u>can</u> do
              – what they will do

Salary
                        Travel
Benefits
(e.g. car)
                                            Action – reply
                                                   – c.v.
                                                   – photo
                                                   – interviews
Special characteristics   – deadline
– clean driving licence
– fluent French
– able to write a good report   Job title
                                           Job objectives ==

                            Main tasks/ responsibilities ——
                                                            ==

Training

What will take most space? What, if anything, should go in an appendix?

Note: sometimes there is a fear that we lack material. The Board, or whoever, is expecting some quantity of analysis, consideration or thinking represented, and we worry we will have difficulty filling three pages. Usually the reverse is true and this is the stage at which to prune, if necessary, so that what is included is well chosen, but not inappropriately long.

This is true at all levels. Contain the number of points to be made and the amount to be said about each. Of course, you need to write sufficient to make your case, but do not risk submerging it in a plethora of irrelevant detail or subsidiary points that are actually unnecessary digressions.

Again the boxed section continues the example.

Stage 4: Review

At this point have a final look over what you now plan to do: review the 'arranged' guideline. It will be quicker and easier to make final amendments now than when you finally print out 20 or 30 pages of draft. It may help to 'sleep on it', carrying out a final review having distanced yourself from what you have done so far, at least for a moment. You get so close to something that you are working hard at, that you cannot see the wood for the trees. One of the things you want to be clear about is the broad picture: if this is right, then the details will slot in much more easily.

Do not worry if you still want to make amendments at this stage. Add things, delete things, move things about (rewrite your guidelines if necessary) but make sure that when you move on to write something you do so confident that the outline represents your considered view of the content and will act as a really useful guide.

It is worth pausing here to recap, at least in terms of making a comment about the process so far. For many a document this whole process (ie stages 1–4) will only take five or ten minutes, and that is time well spent, as it will reduce the time taken once you start to write. As you develop your own style of this sort of preparation, you will find you can shorthand the process a little, with some documents able to be written from the first freehand style list. If real complexity is involved, of course, it may take longer. It is also a procedure that works well if debate and consultation among colleagues is necessary.

Stage 1 can even be done in a group with a flipchart or overhead projector being used to collect the first thoughts.

With all that has been done to date it is now time to write.

Stage 5: Write

What else is there to say? This stage means writing it. Leaving the details of how you use language aside (for Chapter 4), there are still in fact a few points to make here—according to my plan!

First, it is worth a word or two about method. Do you write, type or what? There may be little choice here. In many organisations the word processing computer has moved in and the secretary has moved out. You **type** it. This may take some getting used to, but in due course it has real advantages—at least for certain kinds of writing—and affects productivity and flexibility. Laptop computers have expanded the possibilities here, and anyone who travels on business can, if they wish, work on the move (some of the first draft of this book was typed, on a Sunday between two training course, in Singapore, and some on the journey).

As a considerable doubter when all this started, it is a sign of the change that is possible that I now find it harder to write something of any length longhand than I do to type it. Despite my keyboard skills being less than perfect my thinking is now attuned to the keyboard and screen.

What else might you do? Many still originate something like a report by writing longhand and then have someone else type it. There is nothing wrong with that. One tip: leave plenty of space. For most ordinary mortals, not everything is perfect first time. You will want to backtrack, to make amendments, add or move sections, so give yourself room to do so with reasonable neatness—your secretary will appreciate it, and be able to work from it more quickly. You also need to have a clear way of signposting exactly how you want it arranged. It is easy enough to indicate a new paragraph, but there is a range of other factors such as bold type, indented paragraphs, and so on, that need to be specified accurately.

Alternatively, you may dictate it. With a long document this is not truly good for productivity and not everyone can keep their thoughts sufficiently straight to make it work well; but it suits some people and that is what is important.

One day perhaps there will be computers so sophisticated you can simply talk to them, press a key and be delivered of the typed report just as you said it. Systems are available now that are a step in this direction. We will see; but when they work and the price is right, I will be first in line.

However you opt to work, the job is to get the words down. This is the bit with the greatest element of chore in it. But it has to be done and the guidelines you have given yourself by preparing carefully will ease and speed the process. A couple of tips may help:

❏ **Choose your moment**: I certainly find there are moments when I cannot seem to . . . when I am unable . . . when it is difficult . . . to string two coherent sentences together end to end. There are other times when things flow. When you do not dare stop in case the flow does too, and when you cannot get the words down fast enough to keep up with your thoughts.

If possible—deadlines may have an effect here—do not struggle with the former. If it is really not flowing then leave things. Stop: for a moment, overnight or while you walk round the block or make a cup of tea. Many people confirm that when the words simply will not flow, a pause helps.

But also allow sufficient time, once you are under way and words are flowing smoothly it may upset the process to leave it. If you feel you need an uninterrupted hour, or more, try to organise things that way. It may both save time in the long run and help you to produce a better report.

❏ **small hangups**: on the other hand do not stop when you

get stuck over some, maybe important, detail. Say you need a heading, it must be clear, pithy and make people sit up, take notice and want to read on. You just cannot think of one. Leave it and write on. You can always come back to it (and when you do, who knows, you sometimes think of just what you want in a moment).

The danger is that you dither, puzzle over it, waste time, get nowhere, but get so bogged down with it that you lose everything you had in your mind about the overall shape of the report or the section of it you are working on. This is true of words, phrases, sentences and even whole section. Mark clearly what you need to come back to (so that you never forget to check it again!).

That said, the job here is to get the whole thing down on paper. It probably will not be perfect, but you should not feel bad about that; a vanishingly small number of people can create a document word for word as they want it first time. Practice will get you closer and closer, and things you are familiar with will be easier than something that is new to you or pushes your knowledge or expertise to the limits.

However, some revision is usually necessary; hence the next stage.

Stage 6: Edit

If you have prepared and written well this stage may often be comparatively simple. With something new or complex more revision is necessary. There are a number of points here that help to make this stage practical but not protracted:

❑ If possible, leave a draft a while before re-reading it. You get very close to something and, without a pause, start to see only what you expect (or hope) is there. It is often much quicker to finish off something in this way than trying to undertake the whole job one stage back to back with the next.

❑ Read things over, out loud is best. You will hear how something sounds and that reflects what a reader will feel as they read. When you do this, you will find that certain things—such as overlong sentences—jump out at you very clearly (you run out of breath).

❑ Get a colleague to read it. A fresh look often casts light on areas you have convinced yourself are fine, for no other reason than you cannot think of a better way of expressing it. Some people habitually do this on a swap basis. Because it is time-consuming, they ask a view of one thing in return for doing the same for someone else. This can work well; better if you do it regularly.

❑ Worry about the detail. It was Oscar Wilde who said: '*I was working on the proof of one of my poems all the morning, and took out a comma. In the afternoon I put it back*'. Actually the small details are important. For example, you may create greater impact by breaking a sentence into two, with a short one following a longer one. It makes a more powerful point.

❑ Finally, if you are word processing on a computer, do not trust the spellchecker 100 per cent. Greater accuracy throughout most of a document is matched with a tendency towards errors in things like names. You also have to watch seemingly close words: there/their, effect/affect and the like, as these will not be flagged by most systems either (you may have picked the wrong one, but spelt it correctly).

Editing is an important stage. There is a story told of a now famous operatic singer, invited to perform at a major gala concert very early in his career. He was thrilled to be there, and flattered to find, having sung his particular aria, that he was called back for several encores. He said as much to the stage manager as he was pushed back on stage for the fourth time. 'No, no Senor' he was told 'I am afraid they will ask you to do it again and again—until you get it right!' So too with editing. If you need to read it over three times, so be it.

Of course, you could perhaps go on making changes for ever and finally you have to let something go. But more than one look may pay dividends, and if the end result achieves what you want then the process is justified.

In terms of time, spending time on preparation will reduce

writing time. Similarly it is usually more time efficient to crack through a draft and then make some changes, rather than labour over trying to make every line perfect as you first write. Like much that is involved here, habit plays a part. What matters is to find a approach for working through all of this that suits you; and prompts a thorough job that produces the end result you want.

EXERCISE (continued)

At this point it may be worth looking back at whatever report of yours you had in mind or worked on if you paused for the exercise at the start of this chapter. Take time to revisit the preparation process, following the systematic approach now laid out. You may well find that if you go through it again you will produce a content guideline that better represents your intentions (and a clearer objective?) than was the case if your earlier method was more *ad hoc*.

KEY POINTS

- ❑ Be sure *why* you are writing and set clear objectives.
- ❑ Bear the reader in mind throughout the process.
- ❑ Handle preparation systematically, moving from an overview of possible content to a tight guideline to follow as you write.
- ❑ Try to write uninterrupted.
- ❑ Do not be afraid to edit (or to try it out on someone else).

4

THE POWER OF LANGUAGE

If you undertake to engender a totality of meaning which corresponds with the cognition of others seeking to intake a communication from the content you display in a report there is a greater likelihood of subsequent action being that which you desire.

You are correct. That is not a good start. If I want to say: 'If you write well, people will understand and be more likely to react as you wish' then I should say just that. But it makes a good point with which to start this chapter. Language and how you use it matter. Exactly how you put things has a direct bearing on how they are received; and that in turn has a direct bearing on how well a report succeeds in its objectives.

CULTIVATING A STYLE

It is clear language makes a difference. But this is a serious understatement; language can make a very considerable difference and in many different ways, as this chapter will show.

How you write is partly taste, style and also partly habit. Unless you studied English Language at college or university you may have come across little about how to write, and once in business probably did what many did and found yourself following the prevailing style. How many people faced with writing their first report, and asking what it should be like, were simply given a past one and told 'something like that'? Very many, I suspect, and often it was then a case of the blind leading the blind. It is this process that, as much as anything, has led to a continuation of a common, rather over formal, bureaucratic style that does many a report no good.

How you *need* to write must stem as much as anything from the view your intended readers have of what they want to read. Or in some cases are prepared to read, because—be honest—reading some business documents is always going to be something of a chore; even some of those you write.

THE READERS' EXPECTATIONS

Consider four broad elements first. Readers want documents to be understandable, readable, straightforward and natural. Each of these is commented on in turn:

Understandable

Clarity has been mentioned already. Its necessity may seem to go without saying, though some, at least, of what one sees of prevailing standards suggests the opposite. It is all too easy to find everyday examples of wording that is less than clear. A favourite of mine is a sign you see in some shops: 'Ears pierced, while you wait'. Is there some other way? Maybe there has been a technological development of which I am unaware.

Clarity is assisted by many of the elements mentioned in this chapter, but three factors help immensely:

❑ **Using the right words**: for example, are you writing about *recommendations* or *options*, about *objectives* (desired results) or *strategies* (routes to achieving objectives), and when do you use *aims* or *goals*?

❑ **Using the right phrases**: For example, what is '24 *hour service*' exactly, other than not sufficiently specific? Ditto *'personal service'*. Is this just saying it is done by people? If so it is hardly a glimpse of anything but the obvious; perhaps it needs expanding to explain the nature, and perhaps excellence, of the particular service approach.

❑ **Selecting and arranging words to ensure your meaning is clear**: for example, saying, '*At this stage, the arrangement is . . .*', implies that later it will be something else when this might not be intended. Saying something is, '*about 11.2 per cent*' causes confusion. Is it an estimate as the word 'about' indicates? Or is it as accurate as stating it to a precise decimal point implies? Saying, '*After working late into the night, the report will be with you this afternoon*', seems to imply (because of the sequence and arrangement of words) that it is the report that was working late.

Readable

Readability is difficult to define, but we all know it when we experience it. Your writing must flow. One point must lead to another, the writing must strike the right tone, inject a little variety and, above all, there must be a logical and visible structure to carry the message along. As well as the shape discussed in the previous chapter, the technique of 'signposting'—briefly flagging what is to come—helps in a practical sense to get the reader understanding where something is going. It makes them read on, content that the direction is sensible (this section starts just that way, listing points to come, of which 'readable' is the second). It is difficult to overuse signposting and it can be utilised at several levels within the text.

Straightforward

In a word (or two) this means simply put. Follow the well known acronym KISS—Keep It Simple, Stupid. This means using:

❑ **Short words**: why '*elucidate*' something when you can '*explain*'? similarly, although '*experiment*' and '*test*' do have slightly different meanings, in a general sense '*test*' may be better; or you could use '*try*'.
❑ **Short phrases**: do not say '*at this moment in time*' when you mean '*now*', or '*respectfully acknowledge*' something, a

suggestion perhaps, when you can simply say *'thank you for . . .'*

❏ **Short sentences**: having too many overlong sentences is a frequent characteristic of business reports. Short ones are good. However, they should be mixed in with longer ones, or reading becomes rather like the action of a machine gun. Many reports contain sentences that are overlong, often because they mix two rather different points. Break these into two and the overall readability improves.

❏ **Short paragraphs**: if there are plenty of headings and bullet points it may be difficult to get this wrong, but keep an eye on it. Regular and appropriate breaks as the message builds up, do make for easy reading.

Natural

In the same way that some people are said, disparagingly, to have a 'telephone voice', so some write in an unnatural fashion. Such a style may just be old fashioned or bureaucratic. However, it could be made worse by attempts to create self importance, or to make a topic seem more weighty than it is. Just a few words can change the tone: saying *'the writer'* may easily sound pompous, for instance, especially if there is no reason not to say *'I (or me)'*.

The moral here is clear and provides a guideline for good writing. Reports do need some formality, but they are, after all, an alternative to talking to people. They should be as close to speech as is reasonably possible. I am not suggesting you over do this, either by becoming too chatty or by writing, say, *'won't'* (which you might acceptably say), when *'will not'* is genuinely more suitable. However, if you compose what you write much as you would say it and then tighten it up, the end result is often better than when you set out to create something which is 'formal business writing'.

All these four factors have wide influence on writing style, but they do not act alone. Other points are important. Some examples, based very much on what people say they want in what they read, are now dealt with in the following bullet points. Make your writing:

❑ *Brief*: the gut reaction of readers is to want a document to be brief, but it is not an end in itself—a better word would be . . .

❑ *Succinct*: this makes clear that length is inextricably linked to message. If there is a rule, then it is to make something long enough to carry the message—then stop.

❑ *Relevant*: this goes with the first two. Not too long, covering what is required, and without irrelevant content or digression (*Note*: comprehensiveness is *never* an objective. If your reports touched on absolutely everything then they would certainly be too long. In fact, you always have to be selective, if you do not say everything, then everything you do say is a choice—you need to make good content choices.)

❑ *Precise*: say exactly what you mean and get all necessary details correct. Be careful not to use words like: *'about'*, *'I think'*, *'maybe'* etc when you should be using a phrase that is clearly definitive.

❑ *In 'our' language*: this applies in every sense—it should be pitched at the right level (of technicality or complexity). It should take account of the readers' past experience and frame of reference (which means you have to know something about what these are). It should 'ring bells with them', indeed it commands more attention and appreciation if it gives the impression of being purposely tailored to their situation.

READERS' DISLIKES

Readers also have hopes that what they must read will *not* be:

❑ *Introspective*: it is appropriate in most business documents to use the word *'you'* more than *'I'* (or *'we'*, *'the company'*, *'the department'* etc). Thus, saying, *'I will circulate more detailed information soon'* might be better phrased as, *'You will receive more information soon'*. More so, perhaps, if you add a phrase like, *'so that you can judge for yourselves'*. This approach is especially important if there is persuasion involved.

❑ *Talking down*: 'As an expert, I can tell you this must be avoided, you must never . . .' Bad start—it sounds condescending. You are only likely to carry people with you if you avoid this kind of thing. I once heard a snippet of a schools broadcast on radio and someone saying: 'Never talk down to people, never be condescending. You *do know* what condescending *means* don't you?' Enough said.

❑ *Biased*: at least where it intends not to be. A manager writing something to staff setting out why they think something is a good idea, and then asking for their staff's views, may prompt more agreement than is actually felt. If views are wanted, then it is better simply to set something out and ask for comment, without expressing a positive personal view in advance.

❑ *Politically incorrect*: there is considerable sensitivity about this these days that should neither be ignored nor underestimated. As there is still no word that means 'he nor she', some contrivance may be necessary in this respect occasionally. Similarly, choice of words needs care. I was pulled up the other day for using the expression 'manning the office'. As I meant who was on duty at what times, rather than anything to do with recruitment or selection (which the suggested alternative of 'staffing' seemed to me to imply), this seemed somewhat silly at the time. But if it matters, it matters, and while the way you write should not become awkward or contrived to accommodate such matters, some care is certainly necessary.

There is a considerable amount to bear in mind here. The focus must be on the reader throughout. However, you must not forget your own position as the writer; there are things here also that must be incorporated into the way you write.

THE WRITER'S APPROACH

Every organisation has an image. The only question is whether this just happens, for good or ill, or if it is seen as something actively to create, maintain and make positive. Similarly, every report or proposal you write says something about you. Whether you like it or not this is true (and it matters). The profile wittingly or unwittingly presented may influence whether people believe, trust or like you. It may influence how they feel about your expertise, or whether they can see themselves agreeing with you or doing business with you.

Your personal profile is not only an influence in your job, one that links to the objectives you have, it also potentially affects your career. Surely it is unavoidable that, given the profusion of paperwork in most organisations, what you write progressively typecasts you in the eyes of others—including your boss—as the sort of person who is going places, or not. It bears thinking about.

Certainly your prevailing style, and what a particular document says about you, is worth thinking about. If there is an inevitable subtext of this sort, you cannot afford to let it go by default: you need consciously to influence it. Start by considering what you want people to think of you. Take a simple point. You want to be thought of as efficient. Then the style of the document surely says something about this. If it is good, contains everything the reader wants, and certainly if it covers everything it said it would, then a sense of efficiency surely follows.

There is a plethora of characteristics that you might want your writing to reflect. Ask yourself exactly how you want various factors to come over, for example:

❑ What knowledge (of the subject, the people, the situation) should be evident?

❑ How can your empathy with people (immediate readers or others), and/or interest in them, be shown?

❑ What expertise should be reflected?

❑ How is your confidence demonstrated (or enhanced)?

❑ Does what you say express appropriate clout?

❏ Is your case put over with honesty and sincerity?

✎

_____

_____

_____

❏ Do you seem reliable? (perhaps consistent reliability is what should be evident)

✎

_____

_____

_____

❏ Is your decisiveness clear?

✎

_____

_____

_____

All the above, and more, are worth considering to ascertain exactly how you achieve the effect you want. It may also be important to appear well organised, concerned with detail, or to actually position yourself in a particular role: as adviser, say, or honest broker. Such images are cumulative. They build up over time and can assist in the establishment and maintenance of relationships. Whether such is with a colleague, a customer, or concerned with establishing with the boss that you are a good person to work with (as well as good at your work), then the influence can be powerful.

Similarly you might have in mind a list of characteristics you want actively to avoid seeming to embrace. For example, appearing: dogmatic, patronising, inflexible, old fashioned or whatever, in your job, might do you little good. Some other characteristics are sometimes to be emphasised, sometimes not. Stubbornness is a good example.

EXERCISE

List all those characteristics you want to appear through your writing and all those that you wish to avoid.

If you arrange these in checklist form, having them at the forefront of your thinking as you write will help to you achieve what you want with greater certainty.

Such images are not created in a word. There is more to appearing honest than writing: 'Let me be completely honest . . .' (which might actually have the effect of making alarm bells ring!). Your intended profile will come, in part, from specifics such as choice of words, but also from the whole way in which you use language. So it is to more about the use of language that we now move on.

THE USE OF LANGUAGE

How language is used makes a difference to exactly how a message is received. The importance of using the right word has already been touched on, but the kind of difference we are talking about can be well demonstrated by changing no more than one word. For example, consider the first sentence after the last heading: '*How language is used makes a difference to exactly how a message is received.*' Add one word . . . '*makes a big difference*' *to.* . . .

Now let us see what changing that word 'big' makes: it is surely a little different to say: . . . '*makes a great difference* . . .' and there are many alternatives, all with varying meaning: '*real*', '*powerful*', *considerable*', *vast*', *special*', *large*', *important*'. You can doubtless think of more. In context of what I am actually saying here, powerful is a good word. It is not just a question of how you use language, but what you achieve by your use of it.

Note: no report writer should be without both a dictionary and a thesaurus beside their desk; the latter is often the most useful.

This book has the specific task of focusing on reports and proposals. There is no space for a complete run down on all aspects of grammar and punctuation, though they do, of course, matter and I will make some mention of them. I want to concentrate on those things that can help to create the effect you want.

MAKING LANGUAGE WORK FOR YOU

I regularly see examples of business writing that are almost wholly without adjectives. Yet surely one of the first purposes of language is to be **descriptive**. Most writing necessitates the need to paint a picture to some degree at least. Contrast two phrases:

Smooth as silk
Sort of shiny

The first (used, now I think of it, as a slogan by Thai Airways) conjures up a clear and precise picture; or certainly does for anyone who has seen and touched silk. The second might mean almost anything; dead wet fish are sort of shiny, but they are hardly to be compared with the touch of silk.

The question of expectation of complexity (and cognitive cost) was mentioned earlier, and to some extent it does not matter whether something is short or long; whatever it is, if it makes things effortlessly clear, it is appreciated. If it is both descriptive and makes something easier to understand then readers are doubly appreciative.

Clear description may need working at, but the effort is worthwhile. I recently wrote asking a meeting venue to set up for a seminar arranging a group 'in a U-shape'. When I arrived the arrangement certainly put people in a U, but did so around a boardroom style table. However, I meant a U in the sense of an open U, one that gave me the ability to stand within the U to work with delegates. If I had said that, there could have been no misunderstanding.

Description is important, but sometimes we want more than that. We want an element of something being descriptive, and also **memorable.** It seems to me that this is achieved in two ways: first by something that is descriptive yet unusual; secondly, when it is descriptive and unexpected.

Returning to the venue theme above, I once heard a conference executive describe, as part of an explanation about room layouts, a U shape as being 'putting everyone in the front row'. That, I believe, is descriptive and memorable because, while clear, it is also an unusual way of expressing it. Such phrases work well and are worth searching for.

As an example of the second route to being memorable, I will use a description I put in a report. In summarising a Perception Survey (researching the views that customers and contacts held of a client organisation) I wanted to describe how the majority of people reported. They liked them, were well disposed towards using them, but also found them a little bureaucratic, slow and less efficient and innovative than they would ideally like. I wrote that they were seen as 'being like a favourite, and comfortable old sofa, when people wanted them to be like a modern, leather executive chair'. I think this is clearly descriptive, but it gained from being not just unusual, but by being really not the kind of phrase that is typically used in business writing. I know it was memorable, because it rang bells and at subsequent meetings was used by the organisation's own people to describe the changes that the report had highlighted as necessary.

There are occasions where this kind of approach works well, not least in ensuring something about the writer is expressed along the way. Some phrases or passages may draw strength because the reader would never feel it was quite appropriate to put it like that themselves, yet find they like reading it.

Another aspect you may want, on occasion, to put into your writing is **emotion**. If you want to seem enthusiastic, interested, surprised—whatever—this must show. A dead, passive style—' . . . *the results were not quite as expected, they showed that . . .*'—is not the same as one that characterises what is said with emotion—' . . . *you will be surprised by the results, which showed* *that. . . .'* Both may be appropriate on occasion, but the latter is sometimes avoided when it could add to the sense and feeling.

Consider this. How often when you are searching for the right phrase do you reject something as either not sufficiently formal (or conventional)? Be honest. Many are on the brink of putting down something that will be memorable or which will add power, and then they play safe and opt for something else. It may be adequate, but it fails to impress; it may well then represent a lost opportunity.

Next, we look at some things to avoid.

MISTAKES TO AVOID

Some things may act to dilute the power of your writing. They may or may not be technically wrong, but they end up reducing your effectiveness and making your objectives less certain to be achieved. For example:

Blandness

Watch out! This is a regular trap for the business writer. It happens not so much because you *choose* the wrong thing to write, but because you are writing on automatic pilot *without* thought, or at least much thought, for the detail and make no real conscious choice.

What does it mean to say something is:

❑ *'quite'* good (or bad), or:
❑ *'rather* expensive'
❑ *'very* slow progress'?

What exactly is:

❑ 'an *attractive* promotion'? (As opposed to a profit generating one, perhaps.)
❑ 'a *slight* delay'? (For a moment or a month?)

All these give only a vague impression. Ask yourself exactly what you want to express, then choose language that does just that.

'Officespeak'

This is another all too common component of some business writing, much of it passed on from one person to another without comment or change. It may confuse little, but adds little either; other than an old fashioned feel.

Phrases such as:

- ❑ 'enclosed *for your perusal*' (even 'enclosed *for your interest*' may be unsuitable. You may need to explain why it should be of interest; or *enclosed* alone may suffice);
- ❑ '*we respectfully acknowledge receipt of*' (Why not say 'Thank you for . . .'?);
- ❑ '*in the event that*' ('if', is surely better).
- ❑ '*very high speed operation*' (fast);
- ❑ '*conceptualised*' (thought).

Avoid such trite approaches like the plague, and work to change the habit of any 'pet' phrases you use all too easily, all too often and inappropriately.

Language of 'fashion'

Language is changing all the time. New words and phrases enter the language almost daily, often from the USA and also linked to the use of technology. It is worth watching for the life cycle of such words because if you are out of step then they may fail to do the job you want. I notice three stages:

1. When it is too early to use them. When they will either not be understood, or seem silly or even like a failed attempt at trendiness.
2. When they work well.
3. When their use begins to date and sound wrong or inadequate.

Examples may date too, but let me try. I twitched visibly the other day when someone on BBC Radio 4 talked about an 'up-coming' event. For me at least, this is in its early stage and does not sound right at all; forthcoming will suit me well for a while longer.

On the other hand, what did we say before we said 'mission statement'? This is certainly a term in current use. Most people in business appreciate its meaning and some have made good use of the thinking that goes into producing one.

What about a word or phrase that is past its best? I would suggest a common one: 'user friendly'. When first used it was new, nicely descriptive and quickly began to be useful. Now, I suspect that with every single gadget on the entire planet so described by its makers, it is becoming weak to say the least.

Mistakes people hate

Some errors are actually well known to most people, yet they still slip through and there is a category that simply share the fact that many people find them annoying when they are on the receiving end. A simple example is the word 'unique', which is so often used with an adjective. Unique means 'like nothing else'. Nothing can be *very unique* or *greatly unique*. Even the company whose brochure I saw with the words 'very unique' occurring three times in one paragraph does not in fact have a product that is more than just unique even once. Think of similar examples which annoy you and avoid them too.

Others here include the likes of:

❑ *'different to'* ('different from');
❑ *'less'* (which relates to quantity, when number—where 'fewer' would be correct—is involved)

and unnecessary inverted commas (which are becoming a modern 'plague').

Clichés

This is a somewhat difficult one. Any overused phrase can become categorised as a cliché. Yet a phrase like 'putting the cart before the horse' is not only well known, but establishes an instant and precise vision; and therefore can be useful. In a sense people like to conjure up a familiar image and so such phrases should not always be avoided, and reports may not be the place for creative alternatives like 'spread the butter before the jam'.

FOLLOWING THE RULES

What about **grammar, syntax** and **punctuation**? Of course they matter, so does spelling, but spellcheckers largely make up for any inadequacies in that area these days. Some of the rules are made to be broken and some of the old rules are no longer regarded as rules, certainly not for business writing.

Certain things can jar. For example:

❏ Poor punctuation: too little is exhausting to read, especially coupled with long sentences. Too much becomes affected seeming and awkward. Certain rules do matter here, but the simplest guide is probably breathing. We learn to punctuate speech long before we write anything, so in writing all that is really necessary is a conscious inclusion of the pauses. The length of pause and the nature of what is being said indicates the likely solution.

❏ Tautology (unnecessary repetition) of which the classic example is 'I, myself personally' which is to be avoided at all times. Do not *'export overseas'*, simply 'export', do not indulge in *'forward planning,'* simply 'plan'.

❏ Oxymoron (word combinations that are contradictory) may sound silly—*'distinctly foggy'*—or be current good ways of expressing something—*'deafening silence'*. Some sentences can cause similar problems of contradiction, *'I never make predictions'; and 'I never will'*.

Other things are still regarded as rules by purists, but work well in business writing and are now in current use. A good example here is the rule stating that you should never begin a sentence with the words 'and' or 'but'. But you can. And it helps to produce tighter writing and avoid overlong sentences. But . . .

or rather however, it also makes another point; do not overuse this sort of thing.

Another similar rule is that sentences cannot be ended with prepositions. '*He is a person worth talking to*' really does sound easier on the ear than ' . . . with whom it is worth talking'. Winston Churchill is said to have responded to criticism about this with the famous line: '*This is a type of arrant pedantry up with which I will not put*'.

Still other rules may be broken only occasionally. Many of us have been brought up never to split infinitives, and it thus comes under the annoyance category most of the time. There are exceptions however: would the most famous one in the world—*StarTrek*'s '*to boldly go where no man has gone before*'—really be better as '*to go boldly . . .*'? I do not think so.

Note: if you want a guide to the real detail here, everything from when to put a colon and when to put a semicolon, then let me recommend some further reading. There are a plethora of 'good English' guides, many of them reference books, and something like Bloomsbury's *Good Word Guide* is certainly useful. Head and shoulders above the rest however (if that is not a cliché) and something many will really enjoy reading is *English Our English*. Written by Keith Waterhouse, the novelist and newspaper columnist, it is a real guide, but it is interesting, often funny and projects a great enthusiasm for writing. Buy one at once. It is a Penguin paperback.

STYLE

Finally, most people have, or develop, a way of writing that includes things they simply like. Why not indeed? For example, although the rule books now say they are simply alternatives, I think that to say, 'First, . . , secondly . . . and thirdly . . .', has much more elegance than beginning, 'Firstly . . .'. I am not sure why.

It would be a duller world if we all did everything the same way and writing is no exception. There is no harm in using some things for no better reason than that you like them. It is likely to add variety to your writing, and make it seem distinctively different from that of other people, which may itself be useful.

Certainly you should always be happy that what you write *sounds* right. So, to quote Keith Waterhouse: *'If, after all this advice, a sentence still reads awkwardly, then what you have there is an awkward sentence. Demolish it and start again'.*

However carefully you strive to write clearly and in a way that creates an impact, there are certain special circumstances that will tax you still more. Prime among these is when the report is a proposal and its message needs setting out persuasively for prospects or customers. Your internal communication may also need to be persuasive at times. It is to persuasiveness that we turn in the next chapter.

KEY POINTS

❑ Make sure that what you write is not only readable but is designed for its readers.

❑ Put clarity first; understanding is the foundation of good business writing.

❑ Remember to influence the subtext that provides an image of you, and to ensure it works as you want.

❑ Make language work for you; be descriptive, be memorable.

❑ Make your writing correct, but make it individual.

5

WRITING PERSUASIVE PROPOSALS

Reports can be a chore to write and a trial to get right. But proposals are a different matter; writing them makes some additional demands. How do they differ from reports? In many ways they have all the same qualities. They must earn a reading, they must hold and develop interest. They must use many of the devices already mentioned—being well structured and using language appropriately, for instance—but there is more. They must persuade, they must actively work to obtain positive decisions to do business. As such, they are a key stage in the buying/selling process, and, although this is not the place for a complete description of sales technique (for more about sales techniques see Patrick Forsyth, *101 Ways to Increase Sales, Kogan Page*), some factors are important.

A CUMULATIVE PROCESS

Selling may sometimes be a simple process consisting of one meeting. The sales person meets the buyer and, at the end of the meeting—if it has been successful—the then buyer agrees to purchase and the deal is done. On other occasions it is more complex than this, and more drawn out.

In persuading Kogan Page that I should write this book I had to write a letter, then set up and attend a meeting with the Editor responsible for the series of which it is now part. But agreement could not be concluded at that meeting, a written proposal was necessary; in publishing, such proposals consist in large part of a synopsis—a description of the book, its style, contents and intended readers. This was duly considered, internally, by the group commissioning (or not) new publications, and when a decision was made by that body I was informed of the outcome (a positive one, as it happens, or you could not be reading this).

Often though the process of selling something is much more complicated than this. For example, the chain of events might include the following transactions:

❏ advertising and promotional activity prompt an enquiry from a prospective customer;

❏ that enquiry has to be handled (on the telephone, let us assume);

❏ the prospect is interested and asks for details to be posted (a letter and catalogue, say);

❏ nothing more may be heard, but a telephone call is initiated to revive, maintain or develop the initial interest;

❏ at this point it may be agreed that a sales person visits to discuss matters in more detail;

❏ a sales meeting takes place, inconclusively;

❏ follow-up is again made by telephone and another meeting takes place;

❏ a second meeting is conducted and this time the prospect agrees to consider a proposal—*'let's see chapter and verse in writing'*;

❏ once submitted, the proposal may be distributed to others around the organisation;

❏ more chasing may be necessary, and then the potential supplier is short listed;

❏ next a formal presentation is then requested and made (say to the Board, or a buying committee);

❏ a decision to purchase (or not) is finally made.

It might not be so drawn out, but in some cases even the example above might be a simplification. More meetings may be necessary. Certain industries demand additional stages such as a demonstration or test. And every stage, however many there are, is a form of communication. The whole process may last days, weeks, months or even years.

EXERCISE

Every organisation has their own version of this persuasive sequence. Exactly what is necessary is dictated as much as anything by the customer; it is less something that we decide to do, as what is thrust on us by the buying needs of the customers. It may be useful therefore to compile a list specifically setting out the possibilities for your own organisation to see exactly what may be necessary. This will make clear the specific role and importance of proposals in your situation.

Some stages may be omitted on occasion, but only if this is appropriate for the customer. Repeat business may originate more simply than new, for example, because a customer is dealing with someone who already knows and has experience of them.

Now, with the kind of complexity above (and that of your own organisation in mind) consider this: in terms of quality of action the process is cumulative. Prospective buyers only move from one stage to the next if they have been satisfied by the quality of what has been done to date. Thus, for example, if you send inappropriate or shoddy literature it will be more difficult to tie down a meeting.

There is another consideration here: that of strike rate. Moving right through the stages is time consuming and expensive. So productivity—and sales productivity is a perfectly valid concept—is key. Any stage poorly executed risks the process stopping there. The customer declines to continue the process (they may well be checking out a competitor in parallel, and will continue with them) and all the time and money expended to date is wasted.

Clearly the worst scenario is when business is lost late in this sequence of events, as the whole process must be gone through with another prospect (who must be found) to seek to replace the lost sale. This will waste time and money.

A KEY STAGE

Something of the above continuity may be true for reports also, but it is certainly very pronounced with proposals. Proposals are literally a key link in the stages of moving someone from little or no interest in your product or service to that where they take willing, positive action to buy. What is more they are a link that comes towards the end of the sequence. By that point too much has often been done for sales to be willingly allowed to fall through by default because of poor proposals.

There is therefore a great deal hanging on proposals and they must do their job well. A proposal must not, therefore, be simply efficient and readable: it must be *persuasive*. Somehow, in many organisations, written proposals are something of a weak link. Whatever the quality of face-to-face selling skills, it always seems to be less when something intended to be persuasive is put in writing. At worst, over formality—often coupled with too much circumspection—dilute the level of persuasiveness achieved.

PERSUASIVE TECHNIQUE

As was said at the start of this chapter, this is no place for a complete run down on what constitutes sales technique. However, it is worth digressing briefly to consider certain essentials.

The best, and simplest, definition of selling that I know is that selling is 'helping people to buy'. This positions the whole process which demands that the seller identifies, understands and respects the buyers' needs, and makes their case act to facilitate the buyer's making of a decision to buy,

Essentially selling has three tasks. To:

1. create visibility (no one will buy from you if they do not know or remember you);
2. be persuasive (making what you say understandable, attractive and credible);
3. differentiate (to make your case more powerful and distinctive than those of competitors).

All are important and often, with business justifying or necessitating a proposal stage, the third is especially so. It should never be assumed that business is not threatened by competition even when (with repeat business, for instance) this is neither in evidence nor mentioned.

Selling is usually described as constituting four main stages: opening, making your case, handling objections, and closing. Certainly this is the sequence of a sales meeting. Each stage is worth a separate comment, and the implications for proposals are similar to those for a sales meeting:

Opening

Here the key is to get off to a good start; to immediately impress and begin to create a rapport. This must be done in a way that shows understanding of the customer, and not least that is not 'standard'—nothing puts prospects off more quickly than the feeling that they are being given a practised spiel, without thought, on 'automatic pilot' (the more tailored the product/ service is the more important this latter point becomes).

In a sales meeting there usually needs to be considerable emphasis on identifying customer needs—finding out exactly what the customer wants, how they want it and why. By the proposal stage this will have to have been done, and there must be evidence that it has in the proposal.

Presentation

Here is the core of a sales meeting. The description of the product or service must be based on the specific customer needs identified earlier, and must reflect their priority. This is very important as the same attribute of a product may be interpreted very differently by individual customers. For example, two prospective holiday makers may be interested in the same beach resort; the first for the water sports, the second to recover from an illness.

Making the presentation persuasive demands that what is said, or written, is:

❏ **Understandable**: this is the foundation of any sort of communication and it is as important for proposals as for anything else, more so in some ways as a proposal has to act alone. You are not usually there to re-explain anything complex that the proposal fails to explain clearly first time.

❏ **Attractive**: well described, particularly in terms of 'benefits', that is what the product/service will do for or mean to a particular customer. To continue the above example, a beautiful beach sounds good but it is a 'feature', just a factual statement that something exists. A description that 'there is no distance to go or distractions to your relaxation, as the beach is quiet and very near the hotel' or 'there are boats to off-shore islands where the diving is superb' begins to represent the kind of benefit oriented case that selling necessitates.

❏ **Convincing**: in selling there is always an element of healthy scepticism. Why should people believe every word you say, when they recognise that you are trying to sell the product? You have a vested interest in saying it is good. One way to reinforce the power of an argument is to add evidence or proof, from a source *other than yourself*. This might be anything from statistics (eg independently calculated performance figures) and awards (eg British Standards compliance), to testimonials (eg something based on another customer's use or comment).

It is the totality of the case containing these sorts of elements that ultimately prompts a positive buying decision. But there are other considerations.

❏ **Overcoming objections**: not everything said in a sales meeting is welcomed without comment. Prospects can be thought of as weighing up a decision to buy; for that is what they are, in effect, doing. They want to know sufficient about your case to make a judgement, and this includes not just the good points (the benefits), but an appreciation of any snags. After all most purchases involve compromise (have you ever bought anything that was perfect?). Prospects weigh up these pros and cons and *compare* the perceived balance with any competitor who they will be assessing in the same way.

Objections can be dealt with as they arise in conversation; though not always removed easily or even at all. It is creating a positive balance that matters, and ensuring it compares favourably with other potential suppliers. In a proposal (which may well follow a meeting when reservations may have been flagged) you must anticipate what may be in people's minds and make sure the content of the proposal deals with them. This can mean raising issues which sometimes may appear better left unsaid. The trouble with that is that if the reader says to themselves, 'What about . . .?', the proposal will contain no answer; unless the question has been anticipated and built in. Objections must thus be dealt with as much by prevention as cure.

❏ **Closing:** this is the stage (often, in fact, just a sentence) that seeks to tie down a commitment. It may be as simple as saying, 'Will you take 100 to start?' or 'Shall we agree to get this implemented so that we start next month?', with precise phraseology depending on the nature of the business and the product/service. Aiming positively at obtaining a commitment, whether it is a sale, or agreement to another meeting (ie a step along the way) characterises much of what goes on in the sales process.

While selling, in terms of its individual elements, is pretty much common sense, there is more than enough to it to create some real complexity. It is a topic, therefore, that bears some separate study. So, although the rest of this chapter touches on some of the sales techniques, from here on it concentrates primarily on how to write proposals and the 'shape' they need to be if they are to do their job well.

QUOTATIONS VERSUS PROPOSALS

It may be worth being clear about what exactly is meant by the two words 'proposal' and 'quotation'. Although they are sometimes used in a way that appears similar, in sales terms they each imply something very different.

Proposals have to explain and justify what they suggest. They may make recommendations, they certainly assume that their job is to persuade. Whereas quotations, which are much simpler documents, simply set out a—usually requested—option, saying if it is available and what it costs. They assume, rightly or wrongly, that the sales job is done and that persuasion is not necessary. Many quotations should have more, sometimes much more, of the proposal about them. Here the review is concerned with the more complex proposals, though the principles concerned might act to beef up a quotation.

CHOICE OF FORMAT

There are two approaches to the format of proposals. Sometimes a letter, albeit maybe a longish one, is entirely appropriate. Indeed, sometimes doing more than this can overstate a case and put the recipient off. It is seen as over-engineering. Alternatively what is necessary is much more like a report, though with a persuasive bent. Consider both in turn, and when and why each may be appropriate:

Letter proposals

This is simply what the name suggests. It starts with a first sheet set out like a letter, which begins 'Dear . . .'. It may be several pages long, with a number of subheadings, but it is essentially less formal than a report-style proposal. This style is appropriate when:

❑ a more detailed proposal is not needed, because there would be insufficient content, or an over formality;

❑ the objective (or request) is only to summarise discussions that have taken place;
❑ there are no outstanding issues (unsolved at prior meetings, for instance);
❑ there is no threat of competition.

Where these, or some of them, do not apply another approach is necessary.

Formal proposal

This is a report-style document, usually bound in some way and thus more elaborate and formal. Such is appropriate when:

❑ recommendations are complex;
❑ what is being sold is high in cost (or, just as important, will be *seen* as being so);
❑ there is more than one 'customer', a committee, a recommender and decision maker acting together or some other combination of people who need to confer and will thus see exactly the same thing;
❑ (linked to the previous one) you have not met some of those who will be instrumental in making the decision;
❑ you know you have competition and are being compared.

Note: in many businesses it is common for there to be multiple decision makers or influences. Where this is even suspected it is wise always to ask how many copies of a proposal are required. If you have seen, say, two people and the answer is three copies, maybe there is someone else you need to be aware of and more questions (or even another meeting) become the 'order of the day' before you move on.

In anything to do with selling the customer and their views rank high. What they want should rightly influence the kind of proposal you put in. Ask them questions such as:

❑ How formal should it be?
❑ What sort of detail is expected?
❑ How long should it be?
❑ How many people will see it? (Mentioned above.)

When do they want to receive it?

You do not have to follow their answers slavishly, but must make a considered judgement. For example, if you are dealing with someone you know, they may well suggest not being too formal. But, if you know you have competition, it may still pay to do something more formal than a letter; after all your document and someone else's will be compared alongside each other. In a comparison between a letter-style and more formal proposal, the former tends to look weaker, especially when related to value for money.

TIMING

Timing is worth a particular word. It is naturally good to meet customers' deadlines, even in some cases if it means 'burning the midnight oil'. However, it may be that they want your proposal to reflect your *considered* opinion. Promising that on a complex matter 'in 24 hours' may simply not be credible. Too much speed in such a case can cast doubts on quality and originality. This is especially true of services, and of anything which is effectively bespoke. So much so that it may occasionally be politic to delay something, asking for more time than you actually need to enhance the feeling of tailoring and consideration when it arrives.

So, at this stage you know something about the customer's needs, you know who is involved in the decision (ie those who will read whatever you write) and when the proposal is wanted. Remember Chapter 3 on preparation: add in any time that composing such a document demands you spend with colleagues—in discussion, brainstorming, whatever—and set aside sufficient time to do a good job. Once the document is in the post, then—for good or ill—it must stand on its own feet.

CASE STUDY

A consultant takes a careful brief. They have a good first meeting with the prospective client. A rapport is certainly established and, at the end of the meeting, they leave confident that the prospect believes they understand the problem; indeed this they have checked out.

They ask the necessary questions about the proposal that must now be submitted. They know they are in competition, that sufficient detail is necessary, that an innovative approach is expected but one which *must* fit certain existing parameters. There is also a degree of urgency, not too much—but given the current work load . . .

In the event the proposal hits the deadline, but only just. A week later the consultant receives a telephone call from the manager on whom the decision rests. He has one question of detail. He wants to check whether one element of the suggested approach made in the proposal meets one of the fixed criteria. The consultant well remembers the point, and they turn together to the relevant page. 'It's not quite clear . . .' says the manager; and indeed on rereading it, it is not. The wording is woolly. However, the consultant puts the matter straight, assuring the manager that the methodology is suggested that way *precisely* to meet the given criteria. This seems to settle the matter and a decision is promised in a week or so.

Seven days later a letter arrives. It is polite, it praises the approach; but it says no.

The above case makes a good point. No one can be certain that the offending paragraph was itself solely instrumental in losing the work; but it cannot have helped. There is a necessary attention to detail required here (perhaps the consultant did not have time to get a colleague to read it over), and the focus throughout any such document must be on the customer's needs and perceptions. Certainly once it has gone out then you have to live with it. It is not going to sound very professional to telephone a correction later or send a revised 'page 7' to be slotted in by the prospect. With all that in mind, let us turn to see how the content should be arranged and dealt with in a proposal.

PROPOSAL CONTENT

While the form and certainly the content of a proposal can vary, the main divisions are best described as:

❑ the introduction (often preceded by a contents page);
❑ the statement of need;
❑ the recommendations (or solution);
❑ areas of detail (such as costs, timing, logistics, technical specification);
❑ closing statement (or summary);
❑ additional information (of prime or lesser importance—in the form of appendices).

Each may need a number of subheadings and their length may vary with context, but they form a convenient way of reviewing the key issues about the construction of a proposal and are thus commented on in turn:

Contents page

A proposal of any complexity needs the equivalent of a book's title page. This states who, or which organisation, it is for, what it is about and who it is from. This page can also give the contact details—address etc—of the proposer (which, if not here, certainly must be somewhere in the proposal) and some like to feature the logo of the recipient organisation on it, as well as their own.

This should be followed by a front sheet giving the contents, and page numbers. It may make it look more interesting if there are subheadings as well as main headings, especially if the main headings have to be bland, eg 'The introduction'.

Note: the headings that follow below are descriptive of the functions and role of the sections, not recommendations for headings you should necessarily use.

Introduction

Remember, this is a sales document. The opening must command attention, establish interest and lead into the main text, making people want to read on. As the introduction has to undertake a number of important, yet routine, tasks, ahead of them it may be best to start with a sentence (or more) that is interesting, rings bells with the customer and sets the tone for the document.

Thereafter there are a number of other roles for the introduction, for instance it may need to:

❑   establish the background;
❑   refer to past meetings and discussions;
❑   recap decisions made to date;
❑   quote experience;
❑   acknowledge terms of reference;
❑   list the names of those involved in the discussions and/or preparation of the document.

As none of this is as interesting as what will follow this section should concentrate on essentials and be kept short. The final words should act as a bridge to the next section.

Statement of need

This section needs to set out, with total clarity, the brief in terms of the needs of the customer. It describes the scope of the requirement and may well act to recap and confirm what it was agreed at a prior meeting that the proposal was intended to cover.

It is easy to ask why this should be necessary. Surely the customer knows what they want? Indeed they have perhaps just spent a considerable amount of time telling you exactly that. But this statement is still important.

Its role is to make clear that you *do have complete understanding* of the situation. It emphasises the identity of views between the two parties and gives credibility to your later suggestions by making clear that they are based firmly on the real needs that exist. Without this it might be possible for the customer to assume that you are suggesting what is best (or perhaps most profitable) for you; or simply making a standard suggestion.

This section is also key if the proposal is to be seen by people who were not party to the original discussions; for them it may be the first clear statement of this picture.

Again this part should link naturally into the next section.

Recommendation or solution

This may well be the longest section and needs to be logically arranged and divided (as do all the sections) to make it manageable. Here you state what you feel meets the requirements. This may be:

❏ **standard**, in the sense that it is a list of, for example, recommended equipment and spares which are all items drawn from published information such as a catalogue;

❏ **'bespoke'**, as with the approach a consultant might set out to instigate a process of change or implement training.

In either case this section needs to be set out in a way that is 'benefits-led', spelling out the advantages and making clear what the solution will mean to, or do for, the individual customer as well as specifying the technical features.

Remember, the sales job here is threefold: to explain, to do so persuasively and also to differentiate. Never forget, when putting together a proposal, that you may well be in competition and what you present will be compared with the offerings of others.

A focus on the customer's needs is usually the best way to ensure the readers' attention; nothing must be said that does not have a clear customer relevance.

One further emphasis is particularly important here: individuality. It is so easy to store standard documents on disk these days, and indeed it may be possible to edit one proposal into a new version that does genuinely suit a similar need elsewhere (though double, double check that you have changed the customer's name!). But it must not seem standardised. This is sufficiently important to re-emphasise: it must *never* seem standard in any sense. A customer may well know that you must get many similar requests, but will still appreciate clear signs that you have prepared something 'tailored just for them'.

Only when this section has been covered thoroughly should you move on to costs. Only when the customer appreciates exactly what value and benefits are being provided can price be considered in context.

Costs

These must be stated clearly, not look disguised (though certain techniques for presenting the figures are useful, eg amortising costs—describing something as £1000 per month, rather than £12000 for the year; describing and costing stages separately—such as preparing and conducting training).

All the necessary detail must be there, including any items that are:

❑ options;
❑ extras;
❑ associated expenses.

These must be shown and made clear. I know of one company that lost a contract when one of their executives met the managing director of the customer at a railway station and it was clear that all travel—which was agreed—was being billed for First Class and which had neither been discussed nor specified.

This no place for a treatise on pricing policy, but note that:

❑ price should be linked as closely as possible to benefits;
❑ this section must establish or reinforce that you offer value for money;
❑ invoicing details and trading terms often need including, and must always be clear; mistakes here tend to be expensive

(in the UK remember to make clear whether price is inclusive of VAT);

❑ overseas, attention must be given to currency considerations;
❑ comparisons may need to be made with competition;
❑ range figures (necessary in some businesses) must be used carefully (do not make the gap too wide and never go over the upper range figure).

Look carefully at how you arrange this section. It is only realistic to assume that some readers will look at this before reading *anything* else. Certainly for them there needs to be sufficient explanation, cost justification and, above all, clear benefits, linked in here. Just the bald figures can be very off putting.

Areas of detail

There are additional topics that it may be necessary to deal with here, as mentioned above: timing, logistics, staffing, etc. Sometimes these are best combined with costs as one section. Not if there are too many but, for example, costs and timing go well together, with perhaps one other separate, numbered, section dealing with any final topics before moving on.

The principles here are similar to those for handling costs. Matters such as timing must be made completely clear and all possibilities of misunderstanding or omission avoided.

Summary or closing statement

The final section must act to round off the document and it has a number of specific jobs to do. Its first, and perhaps most important, task is to summarise. All the threads must be drawn together and key aspects emphasised. This fulfils a number of purposes:

❑ It is a useful conclusion for all readers and should ensure the proposal ends on a note that they can easily agree is an effective summary. Because this is often the most difficult part of the document to write, it is also a part that can impress disproportionately. Readers know good summarising is not easy and they respect the writer who achieves it.

❏ It is useful too in influencing others around the decision maker, who may study the summary but not go through the whole proposal in detail.

❏ It ensures the final word, and the final impression left with the reader, is about benefits and value for money.

In addition, it can be useful to:

❏ recap key points (as well as key benefits);
❏ stress that the proposals are, in effect, the mutual conclusions of both parties (if this is so);
❏ link to action, action dates and points and people of contact (though this could equally be dealt with in the covering letter);
❏ invoke a sense of urgency (you will normally hope for things to be tied down promptly, but ultimately must respect the prospect's timing).

Remember that this summary may have to work in concert with the so-called 'Executive summary' which is placed at the start of the document to do much the same job.

Additions

The key thing here are *appendices*. It is important that proposals, like any document, flow. The argument they present must proceed logically and there must be no distractions from the developing picture. Periodically, there is sometimes a need to go into deep detail. Especially if this is technical, tedious or if it involves numerous figures—however necessary the content may be—it is better not to let such detail slow and interrupt the flow of the argument. Such information can usefully be referred to at the appropriate point, but with a note that the 'chapter and verse' is in an appendix. Be specific, saying for example: 'This detail will be found in Appendix 2: *Costs and timing*, which appears on page 21'.

This arrangement can be used for a variety of elements: terms of reference, contract details, worked examples, graphs and figures, tables and so on.

Each of the major sections should be appropriately and, if possible, interestingly titled and you may sensibly start each main section on a new page, certainly with a proposal of any length.

Language and layout are important throughout, and comment about both appears in their respective chapters.

CHECKLIST

Before writing a proposal, or to assist critique one, ask yourself:

❏ Has the appropriate format been chosen (letter or formal)?

_____

_____

_____

❏ Will it meet the needs of all involved (eg decision maker, recommenders, influencers)?

_____

_____

_____

❏ *Does the introduction include*:
  — something to generate early interest?
  — appropriate reference back?
  — clear description of purpose?
  — a clear, and individual, customer orientation?

_____

_____

_____

❏ *Does the statement of need include*:
   — a clear picture of the prospect's situation and needs?
   — specific links between their needs and recommendation or suggestions to come?
   — reference to their decision criteria?

✎
_____

_____

_____

❏ *Does the recommendations or solution include*:
   — clear and specific recommendations (and sufficient options if appropriate)?
   — the relationship of recommendations to needs?
   — a statement of how recommendations meet the buying criteria?
   — reference to benefits (and in the right proportion to features)?
   — evidence or proof to establish credibility?

✎
_____

_____

_____

❏ *Do price statements*:
   — link to benefits (tangible or not)?
   — include *everything* that will affect cost?
   — *not* appear other than straightforward?
   — justify cost where necessary?
   — present them as advantageously as possible (eg amortising if appropriate)?

✎
_____

_____

_____

Does the closing statement:
— offer an impressive summary?
— tie up all loose ends?
— link specifically to action?

✎
_____

_____

_____

❏ What about any final elements? Ask yourself:
— Are all appendices, attachments (eg brochures, factsheets, exhibits) checked and complete?

✎
_____

_____

_____

❏ Is the covering letter really *adding* something to the total message?

✎
_____

_____

_____

COVERING LETTERS

Picking up the last question above, the quality of covering letters is worth emphasising. An example will help make this clear, and also emphasises and exemplifies the nature of persuasive writing compared with a standardised and administratively oriented approach.

The following is a letter that came following a telephone call I made to a major hotel, enquiring about the possibility of booking space for a training course.

A SAMPLE LETTER

Dear Mr Forsyth

Following my telephone call with you yesterday, I was delighted to hear of your interest in our hotel for a proposed meeting and luncheon some time in the future.

I have pleasure in enclosing for your perusal our banqueting brochure together with the room plan and, as you can see, some of our rooms could prove ideal for your requirements.

At this stage, I would be more than happy to offer you our delegate rate of . . . (*so much*) . . . to include the following:

- ❏ morning coffee with biscuits
- ❏ 3-course luncheon with coffee
- ❏ afternoon tea with biscuits
- ❏ overhead projector and flipchart
- ❏ pads and pencils
- ❏ room hire
- ❏ service and tax

and I trust this meets with your approval.

Should you at any time wish to visit our facilities and discuss your requirements further, please do not hesitate to contact me but, in the meantime, if you have any queries on the above, I would be pleased to answer them.

Yours sincerely

The proposal element of this was a bound pack setting out the full 'facilities' (what an unattractive word), with 36 suggested menus, forms to complete specifying detailed requirements, and more. Let us concentrate on the letter. It is not untypical of this field. It sounds well intentioned, polite and it gives a little information.

Otherwise it is wholly awful. Ignoring the finer points, the following come immediately to mind (commenting down the page):

❑ I do not want to hear about their delight (of course, they want my business), starting with something about me, my needs and circumstances would be better.

❑ I am not running a 'meeting and luncheon', I explained it was a training session—this is their terminology not mine (and immediately shows the letter is standard).

❑ It is not 'some time in the future', I quoted a date.

❑ Next, they express more pleasure. I am more interested in what receiving the brochure will do for me, rather than in what sending it does for them (and, yes, people really do use the word perusal in writing, though it seems very old fashioned and would not, I think, be used in speech).

❑ Also, although the room plan is useful, I do not see this as a banquet and the phrase 'banqueting brochure' does not seem right—it is their jargon not mine.

❑ The section about costs begins 'At this stage . . .' which seems to imply 'later we might negotiate something different' (even if they would, I am sure they did not mean to suggest this); and are costs best described with the hope that they 'meet with my approval'.

❑ Offering to arrange a viewing is surely what most prospects would want and should be set out as a firm offer, made easy, and positioned as the natural way forward.

❑ Talking about 'queries' implies fault (better to offer additional information).

❑ The conclusion is weak and leaves the action with the recipient.

One could go on. The overall impression is introspective, standard, formulistic and it added little or nothing to the simple proposals they sent; in fact it lessened them.

So, having been just somewhat critical I suppose I must balance the picture. The following can doubtless be improved

A SAMPLE LETTER: AN ALTERNATIVE APPROACH

Dear Mr Forsyth

Training seminar: venue arrangements to make your meeting work

Your training seminar would, I am sure, go well here. Let me explain why. From how you described the event, you need a business-like environment, no distractions, all the necessary equipment and everything the venue does to run like clockwork.

Our XXXXX room is among a number regularly successfully used for this kind of meeting. It is currently available on the dates you mentioned: 3/4 July. As an example, one package that suits many organisers is:

❑ morning tea/coffee and biscuits

❑ 3-course lunch with tea/coffee

❑ afternoon tea/coffee and biscuits

❑ pads, pencils and name cards for each participant

❑ room hire (including the use of an OHP and flipchart)

at a cost of xxx per head including service and tax.

Alternatively, you may wish to discuss other options; our main concern is to meet your specific needs and get every detail just right.

You will almost certainly want to see any room suggested; perhaps I may telephone you to set up a convenient time for you to come in and have a look. Meantime, our meetings brochure is enclosed (you will see our XXXXX room on page 3). This, and the room plan enclosed with our full proposals, will enable you to begin to plan how your meeting would work here.

Thank you for thinking of us; I look forward to speaking to you again soon.

Yours sincerely

further, but I would certainly have seen something like this as much more appropriate. The greatest difference is the improved focus on the customer.

The letter is important, and more so for more complex situations and more elaborate proposals than the above. It will, if it is interesting, be the first thing that is read. It sets the scene for the rest of the message.

Assuming proposals arrive safely and are read, there is another possibility that needs some thought.

THE PRESENTATION OF PROPOSALS

Some proposals are posted just like a letter; once in front of the prospect they must do their work alone, though they may be followed up in numerous ways: by letter, telephone etc. (persistence here can pay dividends).

Often though it is known that complex proposals, especially those involving more than one person in the decision, will be the subject of formal presentations. These can happen in two main ways:

1. The proposal is sent, then a presentation is made later to those who have (or should have!) read the document.
2. The presentation is made first, with the detailed proposal being left as a permanent reminder of the presentation's content.

If such an arrangement is made in advance, then the proposal needs to reflect what it is. For example, you may need more detail in a proposal that has to stand on its own than one that follows a presentation. It might sometimes be possible to (with the prospect's agreement) delay completing the proposal until after a presentation; allowing the inclusion of any final elements stemming from any feedback arising during the presentation meeting.

Certainly there should be a close parallel between the two entities so that it is clear how anything being said at a presentation relates to the proposal. Rarely will any of the proposal be read out verbatim. What is usually most important is additional explanation, examples and exemplification of what has been written.

It may cause confusion if, say, a proposal with eight main headings is discussed at a meeting with nine or ten items being run through (certainly without explanation). It is helpful to the proposer if the job of preparing the proposal and the presentation overlap and are kept close.

A final idea here may be useful: more than one company I know print out—for themselves—a 'presentation copy' of the proposal in a larger format or type size. This enables it to be easily read by someone standing in presentation style at a meeting. It also gives additional space to annotate the document with any additional notes that will help to guide the presentation along precisely.

EARN ATTENTION

The secret of a good proposal is in attention to detail and care in preparation (leaving the obvious necessity of meeting customer needs in terms of the message on one side). As a final comment I cannot resist referring to the Video Arts training film *The Proposal* (which I can certainly highly recommend).

The film shows a salesman struggling to complete a proposal. He daydreams of the rapturous reception with which the buyer will greet the arrival of his deathless prose and the certainty of an order to follow. But the voice-over interrupts—'*but it's not like that is it?*'—and his vision changes to a less rosy image. This time when his secretary comes into the office to deliver the proposal, we see the buyer (John Cleese) sitting at his desk, a picture of hungover misery. He is slowly dropping Alkaseltzer tablets into a glass and wincing at the fizzing noise they make.

There can be few better images to have in mind when you sit down to write a proposal. If you aim to make your next one combat that sort of barrier, you will have to think carefully about it and invest it with some power.

KEY POINTS

❑ Always remember that reports and proposals are distinct from each other.

❑ Make sure a proposal reflects the identified need of the prospect/ customer.

❑ Do not be introspective; the job is to persuade and this necessitates a customer focus.

❑ A proposal must set you apart from competition as well as say that what you offer is good.

❑ Always link the proposal tightly to subsequent action.

❑ Do not just write a proposal well, package and present it well too.

6

THE CONTRIBUTION OF PRESENTATION

The way a report or proposal looks is important. It influences a number of things, ranging from whether it is read, and how carefully it is read to the frame of mind in which it is read. It should be said at once that prevailing presentational standards have increased dramatically in this respect in recent years. Modern equipment, computers, laser printers and so on mean that very professional results are possible for even the smallest company. If you want something printed in colour, if you want a table turned into a graph of some sort, then both these things and more can be achieved at the touch of a button. Even if there is a learning curve involved, most people are gradually getting more and more able to use the sorts of abilities modern equipment makes possible—even if the technology moves ahead as you watch, and makes it a continuing task.

Whatever the level of complexity you need, however, you should be aware that those who are going to be on the receiving end of your writing doubtless receive other documents on a regular basis. If the standard of those is high, and it is likely to be, then yours must look as good; or better.

Again there is no one magic formula for success, rather a number of different things to keep in mind and a number of devices from which to select. All are concerned primarily with enhancing clarity or producing appropriate emphasis. This chapter therefore reviews a range of overall presentational factors. There is no suggestion here, incidentally, that every report or proposal should incorporate *all* of these. Indeed, such devices should not be overused or the net effect can become messy, and useful emphasis can then turn into something that appears strident and inappropriate.

There are four main areas requiring attention here: the graphics and layout of the pages, the use of exhibits (like graphs or charts), options that suit certain circumstances (like appendices) and the overall packaging (binding, etc) of the document.

HOW THE PAGES LOOK

The first thing to be mentioned here is, in fact,
nothing. The white space of the page is as important as what is on it. If text is densely packed, it seems to have no space to breathe, one thing runs into the next and any intended emphasis is diluted or lost. In addition, it simply looks off-putting and will seem, and be, harder to read.

So the first rule of layout is to space things out. In a long report especially, all the spaces between heading and sections, and even between paragraphs, need to be sufficient to give the right look. Margins should not be set too tight. Remember that many recipients of these documents tend to annotate them. What looks neat and tidy on arrival may look a real mess when someone has been through it to prepare for a meeting, say. Assume this will be done and leave enough space for it to be done conveniently.

Now we look, in turn, at a number of different aspects of what is on the pages and how it is arranged:

Page layout

The specimen page (on p.103) illustrates just a few of the devices that can be incorporated in the layout of a report page. One can easily imagine different styles here, with headings larger or smaller, in different typefaces and so on. These days many such formats can be called up as integral parts of a word processing system; the permutations are numerous. It is also easy to modify such standard offerings, or indeed to create new formats, so you should be sure you select something that is just right for your purpose.

SPECIMEN PAGE

1. INTRODUCTION

This page is presented to give some examples of the many possibilities available. As it needs some text, it highlights some of the key elements that layout can incorporate. These are referred to in more detail in the text.

2. KEY ELEMENTS

Headings need to stand out. It makes it easier to scan a page and pick out specific items or topics. In addition, bullet points are useful to highlight subheadings, used here to flag other ways of creating graphic emphasis:

* **bold type**: items in **bold type stand out** even in the middle of a line; this is not only for headings.

* CAPITAL LETTERS: are also useful.

Alternatively, lists can be made easier to read simply by putting each item on a new line, perhaps started by a hyphen:

– this differentiates points from the main text

– it also groups items that naturally sit together

so that such a list could say: 'There are three key factors here . . .' and number them:

i) first, there is . . .

ii) secondly, there is . . .

iii) and so on.

Dividing a section

Sometimes if the main numbered headings are too long they need to be subdivided. This is easily done with subheadings such as the one preceding this paragraph. Other factors can act in a similar way.

For example, a key sentence may be indented like this, this stands out at once; bold type reinforces the effect.

Shown here sandwiched between lines of routine text, the effect is very clear.*

3. FINALLY

Just to complete, and fill, this page it should be noted that the example given relates to *overall* layout, it is *not* usually appropriate to have so many different devices as there are on this page in such a short space. The effect, if these elements are overdone, can become messy.

* *This could also be in, say, italics.* (Footnotes can be useful.)

Typeface

The options here, again, are many. It may be useful to chop and change in various ways, but using too many typefaces in any one document quickly makes it become untidy.

Most organisations adopt a standard layout (or layouts) and this is something that is designed, not least, to match in well with the style of their letterheads and reflect corporate image and style. A consistent look is sensible if a number of items are all going to end up in the same place, say in a customer's file.

Type size

This can be varied to a greater extent than typefaces. Larger and smaller sizes may be usefully picked to do particular jobs, for example:

❏ larger for title pages or headings;
❏ smaller for footnotes or asides of lesser importance.

Graphic emphasis

There are a number of ways to make a part of the text stand out or, for that matter, push other parts into the background (some of these link to the page layout examples and the reference numbers on them link in here):

❏ CAPITAL LETTERS
❏ **bold type** (which can be used to highlight a word or sentence in the text, as well as for headings: see specimen page)
❏ *italics*
❏ <u>underlining</u>
     ❏ indenting.

Indenting is often used with bullet points, and as well as the 'standard bullet' there are several designs: one to match every style of document.

   None of these devices are mutually exclusive, something can be in **BOLD CAPITALS**, in <u>UNDERLINED CAPITALS</u> (or both) or whatever other permutation suits and does the job.

> Another device is the boxed paragraph. This is useful for asides, something that is not so dependent on the sequence involved, summaries—or whatever needs a higher degree of separation. The boxed paragraphs in this series, and in this book, are typical examples.

Numbering

It is important for readers to be able to find their way easily around a document. Not just through it, but back and forth if they want to locate a particular item.

Pages should always be numbered, probably headings too.

Subheadings can be numbered also, of course, though the use of bullet points may reduce the need for some of this.

Formal numbering can also be used thus:

1. for main headings

1.1, 1.2, 1.3 etc being used for subheadings, or even for paragraphs. (This is not suitable for everything as it appears formal and has a touch of the old style civil service about it.)

There are a number (sic) of ways of numbering as well as 1., 2., 3. These include i), ii), iii); a), b), c); A., B., C.; thus it is possible to have a hierarchy of numbered points without instigating any confusion. Always check carefully and be consistent in the way you do this. Also double check that when you say something such as, *'There are three key points here'* that you do stop at three. This is easily missed as your thoughts run on (if you spot an example in this book let me know!).

The rule here is that complexity dictates practice. If something is long and complicated then the numbering will have to be extra clear. This is also important if you know a lot of discussion will be held while referring to the document.

New pages

You may elect to have each main heading starting on a new page (or not, it can look odd and wasteful if this results in too many white spaces).

CASE STUDY

A firm of architects habitually produced proposals with many—and impressive—illustrations, something by no means unique to this sector of business.

In order to make them even more impressive they doubled the size of their whole proposal document (up from A4). They then checked the response to this with some simple research and found that their carefully prepared documents were not appreciated by prospects and clients. Why not? For the simple reason that they no longer fitted in a conventional filing system. This meant they caused problems and, for all their visual excellence, were too often seen as inconvenient or even a nuisance.

The moral: creativity always needs to come second to clarity and convenience—for the customer. In this case they reverted to the original format.

THE EXHIBITS

Because not everything can be expressed best in words, a number of devices are available to create greater clarity. These include:

Tables

This term encompasses anything that is in columns, which, of course, includes figures. The example shows a typical layout.

Bar charts

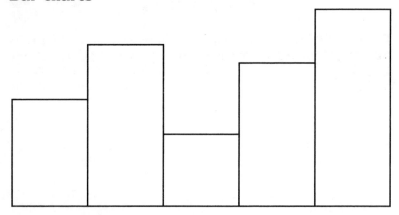

Again the example makes this clear. Be careful not to create a false effect by using bars of different widths.

Pie charts

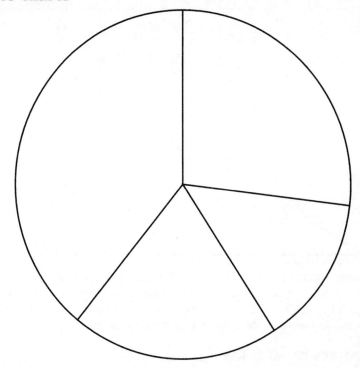

Another visual device that can make many things much clearer than a description or a table ever could. Especially useful for percentages.

Graphs

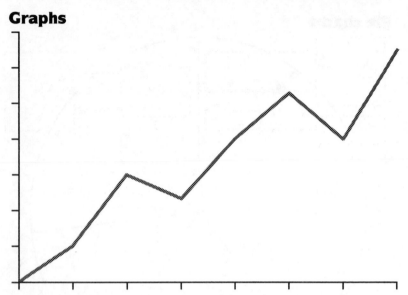

Useful to show the differences of quantities varying over time. Be careful to select scales that give the picture you want (there is a lot of trickery with graphs). It is usual to put the time line on the horizontal, the quantities on the vertical.

Project timetables

A	Phase 1	2	3	4
B	1	2	3	
C	1	2	3	4	5

← ———————————— Time ————————————→

A device to help people visualise the timescale of projects with multiple and overlapping stages.

Flowchart

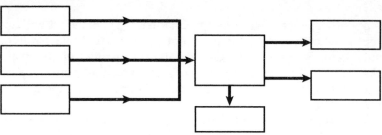

This is more complex, or rather it is for expressing a more complex picture. Best to express interrelationships.

Organisational charts

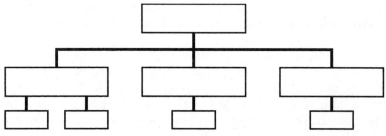

These may represent the whole organisation, or simply a project team. It usually describes a hierarchy, but this need not be people.

All of these devices benefit by being kept as simple as possible. Two exhibits of some sort often work better than one over-elaborate one. Using more than one colour can add clarity (even if other pages of a report are black and white) and is increasingly being used as printer costs come down.

Sometimes there is a compromise here between 'perfection' and the additional time taken to produce exhibits of this sort. If clarity is at risk without them, do take the time; it might make all the difference to the result.

OTHER OPTIONS FOR INCLUSION

Appendices were mentioned in Chapter 5 (pp. 86, 91). I will not repeat what was said there, except to say that the key role of such items is to keep long detailed items separate from the main flow of the content. The more technical and the more detailed such items are, the more important it is to separate them from the main text.

Whatever they are and however many of them there may be, they must be as well presented as the rest of the document. Indeed if they are adding fine detail, then they may need particular attention.

Note: not only typed and printed material may be appended in this way. Additional material, everything from photocopies of press clippings to technical literature and brochures, can be included entirely legitimately. The only criterion is that the recipient will see it as necessary and suitable in whatever form it is added.

Certain documents need an **index**. This is not so common as the need to include a **title page** and/or **contents page** (both mentioned with reference to proposals, see p. 86). The key point to be sure of is that readers will never be flicking to and fro through the pages, wondering why there is not more guidance as to how to find particular items.

OVERALL PACKAGING

Reports and proposals cannot be sent as an unattached bundle of loose papers. How they are secured affects their presentation, therefore the method chosen is dictated by the need to impress the reader.

Convenience is also a factor, and many people favour binding systems that allow the report to be opened and lie flat unaided. There are several options:

❑ A simple report sent to colleagues may only need a staple in the top-left hand corner.

❑ The report can be clipped into a standard report cover or ring binder (one option here is to have a transparent plastic cover that allows the top sheet to be on letterhead or for a smart title page to show through). There are many different types of fastening systems.

❑ The report can be bound using something like a plastic or wire spine with a cover that can be personalised to identify the organisation, department or sender.

There are many options here, so it is partly a matter of taste. However, do not go on using an aged and unsuitable binding machine just because it is there. Select something suitable— maybe you need several different methods depending on the recipient—and finish the whole job off well.

One or two small final points: if the report is going in the mail select a smart envelope if you want that to impress. Certainly select something that will get it to its destination in good condition. Do not forget to weigh a heavy document. If you guess the amount and end up with your best customer paying the excess charge, it will not put them in the best mood to read whatever you have sent.

Think also about the urgency of it—should it go in the post or by courier or some sort of express dispatch service?

If your next important document arrives on time and looking good that is one hurdle over. Beyond that it must earn a reading; and then reward it.

KEY POINTS

❏ Make sure the page layout is appropriate to the purpose and the reader.

❏ Make sure the detail of the layout provides clear signposting to content.

❏ Use graphic devices to ensure precise emphasis is where you want it to be.

❏ Create suitable illustrations (graphs, charts, etc) to assist explanation.

❏ Keep detailed matters separate (eg in an appendix) to maintain the flow.

❏ Package the whole thing for convenience and to give the right impression.

AFTERWORD

What is written without effort is in general read without pleasure

Samuel Johnson

Business writing and the most complex form of it, writing reports and proposals, is not something most people who work in organisations can avoid. It goes with the territory, as they say. Given that it must be done, there are only really two options. The first is to do it well, in which case you will make what you write have the greatest likelihood of achieving what you want.

The second is to muddle through, regarding it as a chore, getting by, and perhaps missing the opportunities the process presents. It some ways the second option seems almost attractive. Some people persuade themselves that the effort of doing otherwise is not worthwhile or is too time-consuming. Some remain convinced they cannot change what they regard as a 'fixed' style. But for most a little thought quickly shows that the second is not really an option at all.

There is regularly too much hanging on the job that reports and proposals must do to treat them other than seriously. If results are not to suffer and if your profile, and prospects, as the writer are to be as you wish, it is something that demands attention.

Of course, it requires some effort, especially if you feel set in your ways. But all the factors that make for success are essentially common sense. Preparation is key. A sound, logical structure creates a core that carries the content and begins to make it clear and attractive. Language matters too. If you have clear objectives and say what you mean, succinctly, and build in appropriate description and style, people are more likely to want to read.

Bearing the principles in mind, any necessary new habits can quickly build up to replace old ones. You will find that with some consideration and practice you will write more easily, more certainly, and in a way that is well matched to your purpose and to your intended readers. This, in turn, will make it more likely that you will achieve your objectives. Even the best writing will not rescue a poor case, but it will strengthen whatever case you put over, making it more likely to be studied, considered and acted on in the way you intend.

With practice you will also find that such writing takes less time. Good preparation particularly can remove the need for elaborate rewriting and editing on material that should have been closer to its aim in the first place, if only it had been given more thought. If writing can be achieved promptly, it becomes less of a chore and this may itself act to allow you to think about it in the right way.

After all, there is a certain pleasure in finding what you consider just the right phrase to make a point; more in finding it has worked and been well received. Professional writers, no doubt, suffer as much as anyone in trying to get down what they want in a way they are happy with. But they also report it to be a satisfying process, even if this is with hindsight: one writer, Michael Kanin, is quoted as saying, 'I don't like to write, but I love to have written'.

So the next document you have to write presents a particular opportunity. Having read this text, you will know something of the factors that help to create good business writing. Whatever your current style and standard, there may be new things you can try, old things you can aim to change and improve.

I will give the last word to an especially prolific author, Isaac Asimov (who wrote nearly 500 books, mainly science and science fiction). Asked what he would do if told he only had six months to live, he answered simply: 'Type faster'. Clearly he was someone who enjoyed writing. But his reply is also a good example of the power of language. Think how much his response says about the man and his attitude to life, his work and his readers; and in just two words.

INDEX